We Are Ready

A President's Preparation and Purpose

Dr. Ronald L. Ellis with
Dr. Mark A. Wyatt

WESTBOW
PRESS®
A DIVISION OF THOMAS NELSON
& ZONDERVAN

WestBow Press books may be ordered through booksellers or by contacting:

WestBow Press
A Division of Thomas Nelson & Zondervan
1663 Liberty Drive
Bloomington, IN 47403
www.westbowpress.com
844-714-3454

ISBN: 979-8-3850-3735-3 (sc)
ISBN: 979-8-3850-3736-0 (hc)
ISBN: 979-8-3850-3737-7 (e)

Library of Congress Control Number: 2024923073

Print information available on the last page.

WestBow Press rev. date: 11/26/2024

Contents

Acknowledgements and Dedication

I wish to express my appreciation to all the members of the Board of Trustees who served during my 30 years as president of CBC/CBU covered in this volume. The support and willingness to allow calculated risk taking has made all the difference in our ability to nimbly navigate the changing environment and quickly fill gaps and impacted areas in the marketplace that fit within the scope of our institutional mission.

Appreciation is also extended to the leadership team who served so ably with me to implement the vision. Special recognition goes to Vice President for Enrollment and Student Services Kent Dacus who has been by my side through my entire time at CBC/CBU. Also, I am grateful for the faculty and staff who readily bought into the vision of building a University Committed to the Great Commission and performed admirably in your important roles. To the students, alumni, parents, donors, and friends of the university, I deeply appreciate your trust and support.

To the multitude of those who taught, assisted, mentored, befriended, and recommended me along life's path, I am thankful. Especially, I am grateful to those who served as my "angels", entering and often exiting just as quickly once their seemingly small but pivotal roles had been completed.

To Mark Wyatt, without whom this book would not exist, I express deep gratitude for your friendship and global travel partnership.

To my two sons, Ashton and Erik, who experienced the fishbowl of growing up in a university president's home, I am so very proud of the men you have both become!

To my wife Jane, helpmeet in every sense of the word and who has stood beside me all the way, I dedicate this book to you.

Lastly, to all who prayed for me during this endeavor and to the One prayed to, thank you 7 X 70!

FOREWORD

The story of the past 30-year history of California Baptist University needs to be written, not just to put the spotlight on the exceptional accomplishments of this fine institution but to try to define the work of people, processes, persistence, and the obvious blessings of God. Having been a student of and devotee of the larger world of Christian higher education for more than 60 years, it has been my privilege to be an observer in meaningful ways as to what went on to create an institution noted for growth, progress, and achievement, and to do that with a deep commitment to the mission of its faith family.

Recent years have been difficult for faith-based higher education. Economic struggles, traditional–age population shifts, denominational tensions, the educational content demanded of today's college graduates, and the cultural values shift in the nation and world are just a few of the challenges faced by schools and their leadership. Reading of historic Christian colleges and universities closing and even of public systems having to realign their institutions makes it even more remarkable when a school shines in dark times like CBU.

To be sure, CBU is not the only faith-based school to thrive, grow and prosper in these unusually difficult times. But it is one of the rare ones whose story can be learned from and some steps emulated.

Unavoidably, it all begins with LEADERSHIP! There is no

substitute for a leader with vision, passion, technical knowledge of what it takes for a university to grow and be healthy, and a contagious work ethic. I have known Dr. Ron Ellis for more than 30 years. I watched him as a young administrator at Campbellsville University help the president move the school from struggling college to growing university. I was so pleased when California Baptist College called him as president at a time when California Southern Baptists were burdened about the future of their college. Some questioned whether it could survive because of persistent low enrollments and weak financial support for years. The school had good teachers and turned out well-prepared graduates. It had hard-working presidents and administrators, but the struggles persisted.

As so often happens with turn-around institutions, God stepped in and led the Board of Trustees to the right man with the right dream, a vision and knowledge of what was needed, and the courage and will to try. Ron understood the importance of comprehensive, highly participative, research-based, long range strategic planning. He surrounded himself with capable people; the state convention supplied him with good board members; faculty and staff bought into the dream; and they set out to plan their work and work their plan. The declaration to be a Great Commission university became the theme and stirred a Divine hand of leadership and blessing to the efforts. Growth, progress, and achievement didn't just happen! It is so exciting to be at a place where the only real explanation to what happens is that "God Blessed! And God Did it!"

Read the book to celebrate the miracle of growth from 808 students to the expected 12,000 students next fall; expansion in curriculum, degrees, athletics, and excellent education; and a significant impact on a major work force. It's also a good read on leadership theory.

Bob R. Agee, Ph.D.
President Emeritus, Oklahoma Baptist University
Retired Executive Director, International Association of Baptist Colleges and Universities

Preface

Imagine it is early morning and you are standing where there is an expansive view. You extend your arm forward and point with the utmost precision at a point on the horizon. You lock in the coordinates and start your journey. The destination, though, is so far out in the distance that the slightest coordinate change could take you off track and land you in a wildly different place.

When I first arrived at what was then California Baptist College in 1994, I had a vision for where we would be in the future. No specific timeframe, but a plan for what the institution would become. I shared that vision as president in my inaugural address at CBC. I have occasionally come across my *We Are Ready* speech over the years and, after reading it again and again at different points in my presidential tenure, am struck by how closely we have stayed to the originally charted course. No matter the unforeseen obstacles we have faced, the coordinates have guided us with unbelievable precision to where we are today – and where we continue to head in the future. We are ready.

INAUGURAL ADDRESS
CALIFORNIA BAPTIST COLLEGE: WE ARE READY
RONALD L. ELLIS
APRIL 21, 1995

Distinguished delegates and guests, the trustees, faculty, staff, student body, family and friends, gathered here on this meaningful occasion in the life of California Baptist College and to me personally, thank you for your presence. Indeed, these are most precious moments we share. Many of you have helped shape the person I am today. You have watched me grow. You have counselled, guided, encouraged, mentored, answered numerous questions, and helped me advance. The debt of gratitude is enormous. Thank you 7 x 70.

As the fifth president of California Baptist College, I am both humbled and honored to be able to help shape the future of this fine institution of higher learning. The founding and history of the College are filled with the spirit of missionary zeal. Today, we reaffirm that missionary spirit as an integral building block for the new era just beginning. May future generations look back on our time and find us faithful.

This institution has been founded and nurtured by those who believe there is a place at the table of higher education for a college committed to providing a quality academic program in a Christian environment. Over the course of the past 45 years, California and the world have experienced numerous changes. But since inception, the core beliefs and principles of California Baptist College have withstood the challenges of the marketplace, the changes continually swirling about, and the test of time. While methods and programs gain and lose favor, the mission of the College remains constant and unshaken.

Each new era is birthed into a unique set of circumstances. In this regard, all eras share common ground. Once begun, the clock ticking without benefit of timeouts, that marvelously exhilarating process of shaping and being shaped runs at a pace and with twists and turns worthy of an Indiana Jones movie. Here at our beginning, we are grateful for the lessons learned and go forth to contend with the pedagogical, demographic, technological, financial, and other challenges to be addressed. These, and some yet unidentified obstacles, are real and worthy of our efforts. As strategies are developed, it is encouraging to remember that within each challenge lies the key to overcoming -- knowledge.

By gathering here today, we demonstrate our belief in the importance of education. Each of our lives has been enhanced by education and many of us have dedicated ourselves to lifelong learning and teaching. More than mere jobs, our professional service is a calling. We are engaged in ministry. Teaching is a great gift to receive and to exercise. Folks involved in teaching imitate the Master and are obedient to Christ's command to "Go...and teach...." (Matthew 28:19)

Out of personal response to the Great Commission, the Ellis family answered the Call to go to California Baptist College. Not to fill a position, but to fulfill a mission. I envision a Great Commission University on the West Coast reaching out to the ends of the earth.

During our tenure (I use the plural because the Presidency is a family endeavor, both immediate and College-wide), the College will be student centered. At the heart of all that the College attempts must be that which is best for the student. Cal Baptist will seek to produce graduates possessing an excellent academic preparation, a Biblically based morality and worldview, a passion for missions, a service mentality, and a strong work ethic.

During our tenure, Cal Baptist will be in the arena contending. We will seek to attract trustees, friends, faculty, staff and students who believe passionately in the mission.

We will seek those who can and will take California Baptist College to new heights, deeper strength, and broader service and influence. Removal of limitations, creative problem solving, energetic and enthusiastic pacing, and openness to new paradigms will be expected.

The primary objective of the College will be to serve the needs of California Southern Baptists, on campus and through extension, traditional and non-traditional, with credit and non-credit offerings. Next, the College will serve the needs of the immediate area and those who seek out our services. Further, the College will pursue opportunities wherever, whenever, and to whomever the Lord leads.

Jesus said, "Feed my sheep. (John 21:17)

Jesus said, "Compel them to come in, that my house may be filled. (Luke 14:23)

Jesus said, "Go ye therefore and teach, even unto the ends of the earth. (Matthew 28:19-20)

Cal Baptist will seek to become the College of first choice for California Southern Baptists. But that will not be enough. Cal Baptist will continue to receive those who come. But that will still not be enough! Cal Baptist must reach out, seek out, and go to all who may benefit from our offerings.

There are thirty-plus million people in California. Over five billion in the world. The population of both is growing rapidly. Cal Baptist will not reach its potential with the status quo. The challenge is not a matter of capability. The technology exists or is readily available. A critical mass of knowledgeable and skilled personnel could be assembled. The infrastructure can be organized and constructed. The pieces of the puzzle could quickly fall into place.

No, the key challenge is more a matter of creating an action-oriented consensus that educating the world is a Christian imperative; that raising the morality level is good for the soul, good for the neighborhoods, and good for nations; that widespread education makes economic, environmental, social, health, and just plain common sense. The world wins. We all win.

The future is bright! At Cal Baptist, a 'Can-Do' attitude is being exercised. The vision is great. The mission is God ordained. The Lord stands ready to bless. By keeping our eyes focused on the Almighty and remaining in His Will, our tenure will have had meaning. It will have been good and profitable that we came this way, walked this path together, and helped build a Great Commission University on the West Coast. There is so much to do and so much fun in the doing. The days, passing so quickly, are filled with excitement, enthusiasm, and progress. Yet we live each day without regret, joyfully anticipating the Heavenly greeting awaiting the tried and true: "Well done my good and faithful servant. Enter thou into the joy of the Lord." (Matthew 25:21)

My family and I have answered the Call. I pledge to give my best as we step out boldly in faith, remain true to the College founders' intended purpose, exercise flexibility in a rapidly changing world, roll up our sleeves and get on with the work at hand. My dream is that this era will serve as a testament to what can happen when a group of talented, dedicated, focused people demonstrate faith in a common vision by their uncommon motivation and productive work. Led by a shared vision, the team is responding, and results are already being seen.

Last night, we experienced a marvelous celebration of gifts. Gifts of music. Gifts of drama. Gifts of art, prayer ministry, service, and campus improvements. For example, Gene and Billie Yeager have pledged $75,000 to construct a 145-space parking lot in front of the Van Dyne Fieldhouse. An uncommon feat has been accomplished this spring. The spring enrollment is larger than last fall's enrollment. And we are just getting started. A goal has been set for next fall that will exceed the highest enrollment ever by over 20 percent. Ambitious? I certainly hope so. Let us be known for setting our sights high and exceeding them!

California Baptist College, we are ready. The best days are before us. Let us be about the Father's business.

As I close my remarks, I express my lasting gratitude to my wonderful wife of 19 years, our two boys, my mother and father, my two brothers, Jane's mother and father, and all my family and friends for their love and support throughout my life. I also publicly express my thankfulness for all that has gone on before at California Baptist College, to the California Baptist College Board of Trustees for their unanimous confidence in me, to my predecessors in this office, to the California Baptist College faculty and staff for their acceptance of me as a co-worker, and to the California Baptist College students and alumni, who have demonstrated and continue to demonstrate that they are worthy of our very best efforts.

Thank you for your presence and participation in this wonderful experience, Inauguration. May we all be found faithful. To God be the glory, great things He is doing.

Chapter 1

Louisiana to Las Vegas

The first years of my childhood were spent in Louisiana, part of the buckle of the Bible Belt. Then from age five to 13, I grew up in Las Vegas where my father taught at Las Vegas High School. When my family moved there from Louisiana, there were about 75,000 people (about the seating capacity of the Los Angeles Memorial Coliseum) living in Las Vegas. By the time we moved back to Louisiana, the Las Vegas population had doubled to about 150,000. Today, The Valley is just one big metropolitan area comprising more than 2.2 million people (about the population of New Mexico). So, it is a very different place than it was then.

While we were in Vegas, we took a couple of trips to California. Little did I know that years later I would return to pursue my life's purpose in the Golden State. On one of those early family excursions, we went to "The Happiest Place on Earth." An outstanding memory about that trip to Disneyland was that the motel we stayed in was adjacent to an orange grove. Of course it was a younger, far less urban version of Orange County.

Another time we went to see some friends who were living in Fresno. My parents, Tommy and Nadine, were up front driving, and my older brother, Vic, younger brother, Lance, and I were in the back seat.

Tommy Edward Ellis and Nadine Craft Ellis

I remember traveling along CA 99 and seeing so much agriculture, one type of crop after another. There were vast fields of carrots and cotton and orchards for miles. There were endless acres of almond trees and lush vineyards, and it just went on and on.

We dipped our toes in the Pacific Ocean at Huntington Beach or somewhere in Orange County on one of those visits. That experience, along with seeing attractions like Scotty's Castle in Death Valley, Calico Ghost Town, and Disneyland, are among my earliest impressions of California.

Basically, I spent the 1960s growing up in Las Vegas. To understand today what it was like back then, I tell people that it was like that TV show, *The Wonder Years.* We rode our bikes everywhere. The things we dealt with were innocent compared to now.

Most importantly for me, Las Vegas was the place where I began to develop spiritually. At the age of seven I accepted Christ and was baptized at the First Southern Baptist Church of Las Vegas, which was the mother church for other Southern Baptist church plants.

We were constantly spinning out five or six families to start a new congregation in the newest subdivision across town. We weren't a very big church, but every 18 months or so we were sending people to plant new churches and do new things. Our congregation's faithful response to the Great Commission had a huge impact on me.

When I was nine years old, I attended Vacation Bible School, which typically is a week-long summer program for kids. That summer, one of our main projects was to make a poster with our favorite Bible verse on it. I chose a bright yellow posterboard and with a red ink marker I wrote the last two verses of the Great Commission from Matthew's gospel:

> Go ye therefore, and teach all nations, baptizing them in the name of the Father, and of the Son, and of the Holy Ghost: Teaching them to observe all things whatsoever I have commanded you: and, lo, I am with you always, even unto the end of the world. Amen.[1]

I took the poster home to the bedroom I shared with my older brother. I had the top bunk bed, and he had the bottom bunk. I taped my poster to the wall above my bunk so every morning and every night that was the first and last thing I would see. That summer Matthew 28:19-20 really became my life's verse.

I sometimes imagine what it must have been like when Jesus spoke those words. Think about it: even after three years of living and being with Christ, after he was crucified, his apostles had gone back to whatever they were doing before. For example, if you were a fisherman, you went back to fishing. Then Jesus summons them to a mountaintop experience and promises they will see him again. Even then there's doubt as they make their way to the meeting place in Galilee.

When they arrive, Jesus is soon to ascend into Heaven, and this

---

[1] *Matthew 28:19-20 (KJV)*

likely will be some of his last words on Earth to his followers until he comes back. What is he going to say to them?

Jesus begins his farewell message by reminding his disciples of his divine authority, and then delivers a timeless global commission to his followers: "Go ye therefore, and teach all nations, baptizing them in the name of the Father, and of the Son, and of the Holy Ghost: Teaching them to observe all things whatsoever I have commanded you: and, lo, I am with you always, even unto the end of the world. Amen."

Wow!

I'm kind of a bottom-line guy and, for me, that answered what I consider the 'So what?' question of the Bible. In this passage, Jesus has given the marching orders for the remaining 11 disciples – I call it a 92% retention rate – and for all his other followers that come in every generation.

That tremendous impression of Christ's Great Commission stayed on my heart as I became a teenager and then a young adult. It remained strong into my mid-20s when I felt a call to do what I'm doing to this day. About the age of 25 I felt called to be the president of a struggling Baptist college and turn it around. Once that calling became clear, I began preparing myself to be able to do that. I was willing to go anywhere I sensed God wanted me to go. The idea was to build a university committed to the Great Commission. So, I have spent my adult life pursuing the Great Commission.

I tend to be a passionate guy. If I'm going to be in, I've got to be all in. And if I'm going to be all in, then I have to be willing to be wrong on this. One thing I tell students, whenever I've given them advice, is think about your life as if you're about to die, and then work back to where you want to be when you reach that point. So, you're now recounting the past as you're about to be going to heaven. As you draw your last breath, what is it that will put a little smile on your face as you review your life? Whatever that is, I tell them, it is how you should live your life from this point forward.

An allegory I like to offer is a hypothetical idea with two different versions. In the first one, I imagine that I have died and gone to heaven where St. Peter greets me at the Pearly Gate. In Option One, he says, "Ron, you're in! But I just want to ask you a few questions." I say sure and St. Peter asks, "Remember back in the '70s when the __________ was all the rage and splitting churches?" And I say, 'Oh that's a bad memory. Yeah, that wasn't my finest hour, I just never ...'

St. Peter cuts me off and says, "Let's go to the '80s. Remember all the controversy about __________ in church and how it caused so much division in the churches and how you responded to that?"

Now I'm thinking, 'Oh my gosh, here we go!' These were situations I had observed in my lifetime, but rather than engage in what I considered faddish events I had chosen not to take part in them, opting instead to pursue my personal BHAG.[2]

St. Peter continues, "And then the '90s..." and he describes another unproductive situation that shifted attention from what the church was supposed to be doing. In this imaginary scenario I realize my whole life had been a long series of controversies that continually distracted me from fulfilling the purpose God created me for.

Finally, St. Peter says, "It's okay, Ron, you're still in." But as I pass through the Pearly Gate, I'm crestfallen, barely dragging along because now I realize what I might have accomplished for the kingdom but failed to do. That is Option One.

Option Two is kind of like a confidence interval in statistics, which describes the degree of uncertainty in a particular metric of interest, typically expressed as a percentage. I am convinced that believers must have faith because we do not know anything with 100% absolute certitude. And if that is so, then what am I willing to be wrong on?

Follow my reasoning here. Since I was 25, I have tried to live purposefully with the idea that I want to spend my adult life building a university committed to the Great Commission. So here is how Option Two plays out in that situation.

I die. I arrive at the Pearly Gates and St. Peter says, "Ron, you're

---

[2] Big Hairy Audacious Goal, from Collins, James C. 2002. *Built to Last.* 3rd ed. New York, NY: HarperBusiness.

in. I just need to ask you one question." I say sure, and he begins, "You spent your entire adult life building a university committed to the Great Commission." Then, incredulously, he asks "Really?"

Finding and pursuing one's purpose in life is an individual choice every believer must make. The choice I made may well surprise St. Peter in my imaginary story. But because of my background and walk of faith, the only thing I'm willing to be wrong about and passionate about is the Great Commission. I'm going to risk it all on that.

Chapter 2

Scouting, School, and Selling Books

I sensed at an early age that the Great Commission would be a North Star to guide my personal and professional life choices. Eventually it would lead me to become president of a struggling Baptist college with the express goal of turning it into a thriving comprehensive Christian university. But not at first. That vision came later.

My mother used to say that from the time I was born, I was leaving. Whether I was going to camps or other pursuits, I was always goal-oriented and through a combination of my effort and occasionally getting a break, I learned that things tended to work out for the best. Having goals, knowing what I wanted, and then going for it became second nature to me. That way, when presented with an opportunity, I would be ready and able to capitalize on it. I'll give you an example.

When I lived in Las Vegas my best friend, Tim Hedahl, introduced me to scouting. He was a grade ahead of me in school, and he was very goal-oriented, so he was a big influence on me. With Tim's encouragement, I joined the Boy Scouts. In short order,

I achieved the rank of Life Scout, which is awarded for earning merit badges, serving in a position of responsibility for six months, and performing at least six hours of community service. Life Scout is the second highest rank attainable, above Star Scout and below Eagle. My goal was to join fewer than five percent of all Scouts who reach the ultimate rank of Eagle Scout.

Then, abruptly, my family moved to Hornbeck, Louisiana, a rural town of 400 residents. My father was offered a teaching job in nearby Leesville, and we moved over the Christmas break because if he didn't accept it then, it probably wouldn't become available again. But when we arrived at our new home in Vernon Parish, the Louisiana equivalent of a county, I was beyond disappointed to learn there was no Boy Scout troop in Hornbeck.

Vernon Parish was home to Fort Polk, a U.S. Army base renamed Fort Johnson in 2023 to honor Sgt. William Henry Johnson, a Black hero of World War I who received a medal of honor nearly a century later. During the 1960s as the war in Vietnam intensified, Fort Polk became the Army's largest infantry training center. More than one million soldiers trained at Fort Polk during the Vietnam War. Soldiers, many of them draftees, trained there for a year or so before they shipped out.

With little rental property available near Fort Polk to house married trainees, soldiers and their families sometimes had to go as far as Hornbeck, which was about 25 miles from Fort Polk, to find housing. One such soldier was Dave Crawford from Kansas, a good looking, folk singing, pre-pharmacy student at the University of Kansas who had gotten married and evidently didn't take enough units one semester, so he was called up by Uncle Sam.

Crawford entered the Army as a specialist, a well-educated guy, and he and his wife ended up renting a duplex about a mile out of Hornbeck. He could play guitar and sing all the folk songs back then and was just a magnetic guy and, as it happened, a Boy Scout of Boy Scouts. He had only been there about a month or so when word spread at the school I was attending that he wanted to start a Boy Scout troop, and was anybody interested? I got back to him, and he contacted me, and I basically helped him start the Boy Scout troop because I was a Life Scout. I understood scouting and everyone else hardly even knew what it was.

Our troop consisted of a Life Scout and a bunch of novices at the lowest ranks, Scout and Tenderfoot. I was in a leadership position right off the bat and I was able to finish my Eagle in a little over a year. We did a number of rigorous activities; we earned a 50-mile patch, completed a 150-mile canoe trip down the Sabine River, and I earned the mile swim patch and the Order of the Arrow.

With Dave Crawford leading us, the troop went from zero members to a robust Boy Scout troop, with me serving in various leadership positions. But then, suddenly, Dave was gone. Within a month or two after I achieved Eagle Scout, Dave was shipped out. Unfortunately, the troop didn't have deep roots. A dad or two took over as troop leaders, but they were unfamiliar with scouting and within six months, I think, the troop dissolved.

Looking back, I count Dave as one of the special "angels" that have appeared in my life at certain times with purposeful outcomes. Dave came into my life at a point where I was probably never going to be able to be an Eagle Scout. He appears and he's there for a year, maybe 14 months, and I make Eagle. Then he's gone.

I never saw him again, never talked with him. I lost track. With my other angels, the circumstances have been different. I will have more on that later. But again, it's a combination of me having goals, being on a track, and doing a lot of things. And when some opportunity comes along, I take advantage of it or utilize it, and it works out and then poof! It's gone. I would say that has been a recurring theme in my career and in my life, always being opportunistic, looking for opportunities.

Another example of this happened later in high school when I sold books one summer. Here's what happened there. Let's just say I was bored at the small school I attended. Most of the students at this school were not going to go to college. There wasn't much emphasis on college preparation. I had a different interest since I was in the fifth grade in Las Vegas, when I began sending away for catalogs from the United States Naval Academy and West Point. I collected the catalogs every year and I pretty much knew the curriculum at both institutions. I read those things cover to cover. I learned all the requirements for admission and my goal was to go to one of those schools. That was my holy grail; I wanted to be eligible for appointment to a U.S. military academy.

I was in the eighth grade at Hornbeck a year after we moved there and as we were looking over our high school schedule, I noticed that the school did not have the curriculum for me to be eligible to go to a military academy. There was no foreign language, no upper-level sciences or math, just basic algebra, and geometry, but no trigonometry or calculus. Nothing.

I realized the required curriculum was not available for me and that was a real downer. By the time I'm in the tenth grade, I just have to figure out a way to graduate a year early from high school. This was before the Internet, and I have no real support for my quest from my school. So, I write to the education department in the state capital, Baton Rouge, to confirm the requirements for high school graduation.

I learned I needed 16 specific units to graduate and after my eleventh-grade year I would be just one and a half units short. I also found out about a university in another state that had a correspondence school program. So, I signed up for one unit in American history and a half unit in psychology or sociology. After completing those and passing the proctored tests, I was on track to graduate after my junior year.

Needless to say, the senior class was not really excited about this, but I just needed to get on with my life and so I graduated after 11 years. That's important because I was still basically taking classes with the 11th graders except for senior English, which I was able to schedule. So, I was taking 11th and 12th grade English at the same time, but I was in another class and kind of bored.

I decided I needed to raise my hand and ask if I could go to the restroom. The teacher said yes, and I began walking down the hall. Now, to get to the restroom, I had to go past the library. Well,

I was not in a hurry and when I got to the library the door was open. Inside I saw five guys sitting around a table, four senior boys listening to someone who I didn't recognize. So, I asked, "What are you guys talking about?" The fellow I didn't recognize said, "Well, who are you?"

I told him my name and he said, "I'm just talking to seniors."

"Well, I'm graduating," I said, and he asked, "Would you like to sit down?"

"Sure," I said, and long story short, I ended up being the only person in that school to sign up to sell books that summer after a chance meeting in the library with a recruiter for the Southwestern Publishing Company out of Franklin, Tennessee. I ended up on the summer sales team comprising mostly college students. But that year, as a 17-year-old, I finished in the top 100 salespeople in the company.

For me, it was like a military training experience, a big step toward maturity. The big thing for the sales team was learning the script. The company provided a lot of positive thinking, motivational material, and then you would go out to your sales territory to work six days a week, selling a set of two student handbooks.

On Sundays, the team would meet and review how everyone was performing. The leader would give out awards and pump you up with camaraderie to get you ready to go out and do it again.

Bookmen, as we were known, worked 12 to 14 hours a day. These are all cold calls where you go and make a presentation. When you get in there, you need to spend no more than 20 minutes and if you go all the way through and make the presentation and the customer asks questions, that counts as a presentation. But if you go halfway through and it doesn't look good, you try to close it up and you don't count that one. If you were good at it, you would make 30 complete presentations a day and sell 10 sets of books.

After a month or six weeks I got to where I could do that. And if I had three prospects in a row that didn't buy, I would almost be running to the next one because I knew the probability was that I was about to close a sale.

Selling books also taught us how to limit expenses. Bookmen were paid only on commission and lived off deposits. Each salesperson was basically running his own business. We were selling the book set for just under $25 and tried to get a five-dollar deposit. The larger the deposit, the more likely the customer would pay for the books on delivery. As a seller, you don't want to take anything less than $2. You try to get $5; $10 is great. And if the customer wants to pay for the whole thing, that's even better. But you're going to do all this accounting when you get back to your shared rental and then you get up the next morning and do it again.

Sales team members are not supposed to knock on a door until eight o'clock. So, you're sitting out there at 7:30, watching your clock. And if you could bum sandwiches and do things like that, that's just food you don't have to buy. They have competitions to see who spent the least amount of money. So, you're bumming drinks and you've got somebody looking at you, you're a little skinny thing and they say, "Hey, would you like a salad?"

"Yes, ma'am, I would."

And so, you really learned important lessons: maximize revenue, limit expenses. You're running your own company.

Then at the end of the summer, you order your books and now you're going to deliver them. So, you're delivering your books and guess what? Some people have moved. You don't know where they are. Some people refuse to take them. And so now you have to sell that book or ship it back and if you ship it back, it's on you. So, you're losing double. And then the last thing you do is you go back to Franklin, Tennessee and they cash you out and you receive your check. Through the summer you have been sending in the money and so you square up with the company. Remember, this is 1973, and I earned a check for $3,300 after expenses. A schoolteacher in Louisiana at that time was probably making about $5,500 to $7,000. Minimum wage was about $1.60 an hour. So, $3,300 in three months was a lot of money.

The first thing I did when I returned home was tithe on my summer income. Selling books was a great experience because you had to be self-disciplined. You're only going to earn what you kill, so to speak, and then what you don't spend. You learn the whole package about how to run a business, be self-motivated. You're selling and there's no selling like cold selling. I mean, knocking doors and how many times you're going to get that door slammed in your face; or you hear the TV, and they look through the blind, but they aren't opening the door. Even if you make 30 quality presentations, you're going to sell 10 sets, so there's two-thirds rejection right there. So, you have to be in a total positive frame of mind that 'I can do this.'

And another thing: the company wouldn't let you sell in a state adjacent to your home state. I'm from Louisiana so I'm assigned to eastern Tennessee by design. The company doesn't want you working close to where you live so you can't just go home. You can't see anybody. Nobody from your home can come to visit you. You can talk to them on the phone, but that's it. So, what happens is this: probably 80% of everybody who's not going to be there at the end of the summer is already gone in the first or second week, because either you can do this, or you don't.

About my third day on the job, I just couldn't sell. I think I sold one set a day. But then our supervisor, Roddy Dye, a great sales guy from Louisiana, came and spent about three hours with me. During his time with me, he would make a presentation, and I would watch. Then I would do one and he would watch. Afterward, we talked about it and then we'd do it again. What was great is that he made a sale on his first presentation. I don't think I sold my first one, but I was close.

Then Roddy sold his second set. Then, on my second presentation, I sold one. After that, I was sailing. I didn't need more coaching. I was 98% right and I think it was probably more a matter of confidence than anything else. Whatever it was, once that occurred my sales percentages went up and up. I was getting in the door more often and everything was just rolling.

By the time I had been doing this for four weeks, I was a machine. I mean, I was totally locked in, totally focused. People may have noticed a similar focus during my years at California Baptist

University. When I get locked in on something like enrollment, I am all in. It's what I do. And that whole summer, selling books in the Volunteer State, I would say by the time I'd been there three or four weeks, I was so locked in on it nothing else even mattered.

Here's another thing about this idea of opportunity. When Dave Crawford put out a call for boys interested in scouting in Hornbeck, I could have said, "I'm too busy, I'm beyond that." But I didn't. When that opportunity came in, I was all in, 100%.

It was the same thing with selling books. I'm going down to use the bathroom, just to get out of class, and I see these guys over there talking in the school library. The door is open, so I go over and put myself into the conversation and end up going to sell books over the summer. In other words, the theme is all about opportunity, seeing it and acting on it.

That theme is continuing to play out here at California Baptist University, like when I was on a plane one day and in the pouch in front of my seat there was a business magazine, either Forbes or Fortune. On the cover was a headline about a coming pilot shortage. Well, I read the article and today we have a robust aviation science program at CBU.

I think that has been a significant theme for me, that I continually look for opportunities and whenever I decide to seize an opportunity, I run with it. When that happens, I've got to do a lot of work and that's fine. I just need the opportunity.

Chapter 3

Northwestern State University Black Knights Drill Team

I finished high school in 1973, a year early, and took a summer job selling books door-to-door in Tennessee for Southwestern Publishing Company. I did quite well at that job, and that fall I enrolled at Northwestern State University (NSU), the regional university for people living in that largely rural part of Louisiana.

I missed city living and the more dynamic, cosmopolitan lifestyle I had experienced from the ages of 5 to 13, growing up in Las Vegas. Consequently, I wasn't all that excited about attending Northwestern State University, but I was determined to make the best of it.

At NSU, I joined ROTC and the Black Knight Drill Team that appeared in a number of parades and other events including the Rex Mardi Gras parade in New Orleans.

For me, another memorable highlight was a performance at the Los Angeles Rams-New Orleans Saints NFL pregame show at Tulane Stadium two years before the Superdome was opened.

I will never forget that experience. There were 16 of us, four rows of four cadets wearing white gloves and taps on our boots, drilling with hefty M16 military rifles fitted with bayonets. We performed a three-to-five-minute silent drill, and I vividly remember walking out onto the field before the televised game to perform the drill and then exit before the National Anthem.

Black Knights

Northwestern's Black Knights Drill Team existed as an integral part of the Reserve Officers Training Corps. This precision marching team was organized to provide leadership training, foster the development of discipline and to encourage competitiveness. Membership was open to any member of the ROTC in satisfactory standing with the ability to perform according to the standards of the Black Knights.

Northwestern's Black Knight Drill Team

It's a big game. There are 66,000 people packed in the stands and as the Black Knights are announced, it seems nobody stops talking or even takes notice. Everybody continues milling around, doing this and that while we march out to almost center field as one unit, each team member acutely aware that every step taken is not just you, but the whole drill team.

As we approach the center of the field, the crowd noise starts falling like somebody is turning down the volume control and the crowd begins to look at us, as if wondering, 'What is this?'

We form a circle for the opening drill at mid-field and begin our highly polished routine, each cadet tapping his weapon twice and then throwing it. The weapons spin and fly across the circle and our job is to move as little as possible, catch the rifle, bring it down, and then repeat the maneuver. We perform several throws just like that, the cadets all earnestly hoping that if anybody drops a weapon it won't be them.

That day I think we were flawless. It was fantastic, probably one of the best performances we ever did. Everything went off exactly as planned. Following the opening circle ring we performed other precision drills, all with not a single word being spoken. That's impressive when the audience realizes there is no one giving an order through the entire presentation.

We conclude our routine with a kneeling Queen Anne Salute, the cadets dropping to one knee in unison and holding in place for a count of eight. When the leader taps twice, the team comes up as one, spinning their weapons onto their shoulders, every move done on silent counts. Again, the team holds in place for a predetermined count before marching off the field to a smattering of appreciative applause. But by the time we were off the field, people were shouting and cheering our performance.

Reaching the sidelines we were drenched in sweat. First, it's Louisiana; but also, the adrenaline could not have been higher. And of course, all our families back home were watching their TVs. It was a time before mobile phones and instant communication, so when I finally got to a landline and I could call home, I asked, 'How did it look? We performed our drill before the national anthem, okay?'

"Well," they replied, "the telecast went live at the national anthem. Where were you guys?"

At that moment, I realized that 66,000 people packed into Tulane Stadium saw the drill team performance, but nobody in the TV audience did. That was disappointing, but still it was a great experience.

Another disappointment befell our Black Knight drill team the following spring. One of the major events the Black Knights prepared for every year was a massive competition in Washington,

DC known as the National Cherry Blossom Festival Drill Meet. Participating teams stayed at military barracks, and our team was eager to compete against West Point and other fantastic ROTC drill teams from across the country. The Black Knights from NSU were a top five team in the country, and our excitement grew daily as we fine-tuned our performance in preparation for the upcoming drill competition.

However, that year the drill meet unexpectedly was canceled. It was absolutely devastating, similar, I thought, to the way qualified athletes must feel who cannot compete in the Olympics through no fault of their own. It was just so upsetting that our event was canceled and there was nothing we could do.

That experience really soured my time at Northwestern State University because the Black Knights were like my fraternity. The drill team performance was my competitive sport. The team was my community, and we were all disoriented by the cancellation. Suddenly, we had no reason to practice anymore because that was the end of it; there were no more parades or competitions. It was a shattering thing to take.

Chapter 4

From Hornbeck to Houston

I met my future wife the summer before my final year in high school. Jane Dowden had gone with her mother, Pauline "Polly" Polk Dowden, and her father, the Rev. William Roy Dowden, when he interviewed to become pastor of the First Baptist Church of Hornbeck.

Rev. William Roy and Pauline "Polly" Polk Dowden

Jane's sister, Susan, was away at college and unable to join the rest of the family on the visit. The eventual church vote that called "Brother Roy" to Hornbeck would have a profound and enduring impact on my life.

Jane and I began dating about halfway through her sophomore year at Hornbeck High School. I was completing the courses I needed to graduate a year ahead of schedule. I planned to enroll at Northwestern State University in Natchitoches, Louisiana, less than 50 miles from Hornbeck. But I would spend my last summer before college earning some money, selling books door-to-door in Tennessee.

Before I left Hornbeck for that summer job out of state, Jane told me she was going to write me a letter every day while I was away. Sure, she will, I thought. Well, as it turned out, she did! I received a letter from her every day except Sunday the whole summer. I am a bit embarrassed to admit that I did not exactly reciprocate, at least not with the same frequency. I wrote a letter every now and then while staying keenly focused on learning—and earning—during my inaugural season as a cold call, door-to-door book salesman.

That fall, I went off to Northwestern for a year to begin my higher education experience. In addition to my other course work, ROTC drills and appearances combined to create a demanding schedule. As a result, I managed to see Jane only a couple of times a month during my freshman year at NSU.

After that first year in college, I decided to put to good use what I had learned selling books the previous summer. I was going back for more. I told some of my high school and college classmates about the opportunity to make good money and persuaded several of them to sign up for the adventure. We were selected for one of the Southwestern Publishing Company's new product lines, a large single-volume offering instead of the two-book set I had sold before. The marketplace also changed from the previous year. Instead of returning to Knoxville, home to the University of Tennessee, the Tennessee Valley Authority and nearby Oak Ridge National Laboratory, my crew was assigned a territory near Fenix

City, Alabama, a mostly blue-collar area not far from Fort Benning, Georgia.

In Knoxville we had had little trouble selling books, thanks to the region's comparatively high educational standing and good paying jobs. People there really cared about their kids' education and had disposable income. Selling even a $23 product was not that difficult. One technique we used was to inform prospective buyers which of their neighbors had just bought the two-volume student handbook. And as often as not, they would reply, "Well then, we will get a set."

This time it was different. The target market included a lot of soldier types, blue collar workers, and residents who were less likely to buy an educational product than the professors and others who worked at a university or a government agency. Oh, and by the way, this product was almost twice as expensive and featured just one volume instead of two! It felt as though the odds were stacked against us.

Additionally, this time I was supervising three or four of my friends. In Franklin, my first year, all I did was learn the sales script and how to deal with objections, so I was completely focused on that. Now, I have supervisory responsibilities and must ensure my crew members are taken care of. Consequently, I'm not learning my new script like I did previously. Normally it wouldn't be a problem because I would already have done this thing a thousand times. Even having to do the added supervisor's things normally would not be a problem because I would already know the material I'm now supposed to be learning. But I found myself struggling under the new situation.

After completing the week of training in Franklin, we were driving in a caravan to our sales territory where we had found a place to rent. It's late at night, we've got four or five cars in a caravan and as we got close to our destination, we crossed the county line and were pulled over by the police. This is a different era. None of us have license plates from this area. We're all from Louisiana, we're all young men, we're wearing shorts and flip flops, driving late at night and so we're very suspicious to them.

I think what had happened was, we'd stopped to get gas and some Cokes and snacks, and somebody called the police on us even though we hadn't done anything. We just weren't from around here and we were probably being silly, so we were pulled over late at night and they took down all our names.

After that, we just ran into problems everywhere. It's like they had put out an alert about us. I remember not long into my second week there I was sitting on a porch swing, presenting my sales pitch to a lady when two police cars pulled up and the officers wanted to question me. They were asking about one of my crew members, but every neighbor on the street came out to see what was happening. Well, that killed any potential sales and not just that block, but also everybody they go to church with. I answered a few questions, and nothing came of it. But it absolutely killed my market.

One thing after another happened like that, and we could not sell books there. We weren't that familiar with the product, the product was expensive, the market was not that favorable, and everywhere we went people just got up and walked away. You could almost see people saying, "That's a gang from out of state." People wouldn't even open their doors. It was a disaster.

One of my sales crew, a friend who went to church with me, was arrested and put in jail. It was a nightmare. I can't recall the alleged offense; it might have been trespassing or that kind of thing. Whatever it was, we were in a nightmare zone. I'm all of 18 years old in the early '70s. I graduated high school at 17 and went and sold books, so I was very young even for that. Now I'm in my second year, only 18, and I'm dealing with all this stuff. So, I had to go get my crew member out of jail. I had to bail him out. Believe me, that messed up the whole day.

It was a totally different experience than I had the year before, when I was selling books in a really good area. This time, the guys were not selling and one by one they were fired. The way you found out you were being fired was, you went to the Sunday rally meeting. Usually, this was a motivational session where everybody was getting psyched up for the next week and being given awards.

We were at a Sunday rally meeting with about 40 bookmen who were assigned to the area. A short time into the rally, I was called outside, and our supervisor said, "We're going to fire so-and-so." This was my buddy from high school, and they wanted me to do it. I said, 'I can't, I can't.' They said, "Okay, we'll do it." They called him out of the rally, and the supervisor read him the riot act. He told him, "You're out, you're not working here anymore, give me the books."

I had just one experience after another like this that I had never had before. It was like drinking through a fire hose. When my first buddy was fired, I knew we weren't selling. Nobody else was selling this book either but we were really sucking wind, and we had all these other issues. Everything that went right the year before now was going wrong and I couldn't foresee any of this.

Moreover, I have nobody to share it with because my family is not the kind of family you call about problems unless you're dying. Even then, if it is a long-distance phone call, you keep it short. And so, I'm processing all this on my own.

Through it all I'm learning and growing, but it's tough. Then a couple of my crew quit right there. Once the first guy was fired, the others quit within a week. Now I'm the only guy remaining from the crew, and I am thoroughly messed up. I don't know this stuff, I can't sell this book, and even if I knew the script I cannot be sure how effective I could be.

I talked to the company, and they moved me to another location. I stayed about four days, but I was just not into it. I didn't last the season; it was maybe three weeks, four weeks tops, because in these jobs you either get it or you don't. So, I went to Franklin and cashed out and went home. It was just a disaster.

My family had this thing that when something bad happened, for three days you get to be in the fetal position, and they'll take care of you. But after three days, you have to get up and get over it and move on. I went home and stayed about a week and for three days, slept, ate and thought about my life. What am I going to do?

This was still summertime between my first year at Northwestern and what would have been my sophomore year. But I decided not to go back to Northwestern. I've got to have a change, I thought. I needed to work, but where? I knew I didn't want to stay in Hornbeck. There was nothing for me to do there.

Jane's grandparents lived in Houston, and I knew them.

Wayne and Nina Polk, Jane's grandparents

So, I went there and stayed with her grandparents. They had a three-bedroom house. As I was trying to figure out what to do, I went to see one of my mother's nephews who lived in the area and I said, 'I just need some work.'

We get the Houston Chronicle out and we're going through the want ads, literally, and there's a job listed for collections. I just need a job, so I go downtown to apply. If you had a pulse, you were hired on the spot. There are people there working by the hour. I worked there for a little less than a month. You're just cold calling people and harassing them to pay. I hated every minute of this job. I'm thinking, 'Oh man, this is a terrible job.'

I'm looking at the want ads every day and I found this job at Entex, a Houston energy company. Now, Jane's grandparents were the nicest people, but not the kind of people who get asked for advice.

They were older. My cousin, on the other hand, seemed to know what he was doing. He's probably 35 and he lives in a big city, and he knows how it works.

I talked to my cousin, and I said, what do you think about this Entex listing? He said, "Yeah, that's a good job."

I said, 'Well, what do you think I should do?'

"Go interview for it," he said. "Just tell your boss you're sick or something."

I followed his advice. The company was a few blocks over, so I went in. What a great organization! Entex was a big gas company serving a region all over Texas. I went in for an interview and they almost instantly recognized me as a guy with an up arrow. They hired me. I called my collection job and just told them where to send my check. I didn't even go back.

I started the job at Entex the next day. They trained me to read gas meters, and I absolutely loved it. A route paid for eight hours' work, so even if you read a route in four hours, you received eight hours' pay. Certain routes were easier to read, and you could save those for Saturdays and get rewarded. A typical Saturday route consisted of reading 180 meters in a ward with shotgun houses and clusters of eight to 20 meters. At time and a half pay on Saturdays, you'd earn the equivalent of three days' pay by reading two routes, compared with one day's pay for reading a route on a weekday.

Reading meters required recording the value on each of four dials. Once you got the hang of it, reading the meter became a matter of glancing at dial positions, not numerals. By seeing the position of each dial, you would know the corresponding number. With practice, motivated guys like me learned to quickly read a lot of meters that way and take extra routes. What else was I going to do?

With my new job at Entex going well, I moved from the bedroom at Jane's grandparents' home to share a furnished apartment with her cousin's boyfriend. I paid him my half of the rent. But after about two months, I came back to the apartment one day and there was no furniture. I didn't have any furniture; it was his, and suddenly he and the furniture were gone.

I went to the apartment manager's office to see what was going on and learned that evidently, my roommate had joined the Navy without telling anybody. And worse, he hadn't been paying the rent, which I now had to make up as well as getting some furniture. The apartment manager called my roommate's parents who were surprised by what he had done and reimbursed me for half of the back rent. We changed the rental to my name, making me solely responsible for the rent.

Jane's grandparents generously opened their storage shed and provided me with a small table with two chairs, an old couch, a mattress, and a radio. That was it. That was my home.

It may be hard for some people to understand this today, but it didn't cross my mind to ask my parents for money or any other help. I just thought, 'I'm 18, I'm a grown man, so I'm just making it happen.' The good news is, I felt advanced, even going off for the summer and selling books. It was just a different era. I was confident that I could make it. After my first summer selling books, I told some people, 'You could blindfold me, take all my money and everything, drop me in Seattle and I will make it. I will live under a bridge. I will find a leaf rake and I will go to people's homes, and I will rake their yards. Then I will save up and buy a lawnmower.' I had that much confidence in my ability to live and make it in the world. This was my mentality, and at that time you could do something like that.

As I relocate to Houston, that's my mindset. I'm not focused on college at this point. I need to eat and I'm okay with it. I'm not complaining; more like 'Let's get it on baby.'

So, I'm reading my route daily and two on Saturdays because I have nothing else to do. I have no family to go home to in the area, so I'm just working and thinking. On that job at Entex, I usually worked by myself. I would jump in and out of people's backyards all day and then I would come home, and I would be alone. I didn't have a TV, just the radio that I kept on the floor next to the mattress where I slept.

By now it's fall and I'm still not back in college, just working and going to church mostly by myself. I tell people, 'I know what it's like to be alone in a city of three million people. You can be totally alone.' I'm still functioning, but I'm just a shell. I find myself working, sleeping, getting up and doing it again. Wash, rinse, repeat. So, I had a lot of time to think about where my life is going.

I'm making good money at Entex, so I'm doing fine financially. I'm knocking it out, you know, paying my basics and just saving money. I don't eat out, I just go to the grocery store, buy potato chips and a loaf of bread and make sandwiches. But with so much time to think about what I'm doing, I develop kind of a spiritual focus, and I get to the point where I'm praying a lot, talking to God, and thinking about what I am going to do with my life.

I don't feel defeated. I know I'm going to be a leader. The question is which route do I take? I know the military is not going to work for me because I would need to be an officer and that did not work out. I was in ROTC at Northwestern State University, but then the Vietnam war ended, and they basically told us they were going to reduce the army by 400,000 soldiers. It was not a good time to begin a military career.

Okay, so that didn't work out. Next. The academy part didn't work either, at first. But that's okay. The book selling worked and then it didn't. That's fine, too. I'm very open to discovering what is going to work.

So now, Entex wants me and I'm doing a good job, so they keep promoting me, which I soon learned was not as good as it first seemed to be. They gave me a car route and I received a small premium for this in my paycheck. But I also had to shuttle several co-workers to and from their routes. The first thing the guys I was assigned wanted to do when we went to an area was head to a fast-food place for breakfast.

No! I preferred to get ready and once I got the signal to go, I'm jumping into backyards. The other guys, not so much. And then they're going to take a lunch break.

Oh, my goodness! I just wanted to be done by noon and then we're out!

One day we finished our routes and headed back to the office. As usual, we were on the freeway in the big four-door company sedan marked with "Entex" signs and I was driving. I smelled something and looked in the rear-view mirror to see two of the older guys toking in the back seat. I didn't say anything, but back at the office I told my boss, 'I'm not turning anybody in, I'm just telling you I cannot do this anymore. I can't be dropping people off.' I gave him a lot of reasons and I ended with, '…and there may be some activity going on that I'm not going to be a part of. I could be arrested for this.'

The company responded by giving me a truck in place of the car, which was good and bad because in the truck you're by yourself, but you go way out of town and read rural routes and commercial routes. A typical route may be only 40 or 50 meters, but it can take an hour just to get there, and then you have to unlock a gate and, oh yeah, there's a bull in the pasture! Now you have to go find the meter and that may take you 20 minutes to read just one. Then you come back and lock everything up, follow all these instructions and drive off to find the next one.

Sometimes you have to clean the meters before reading them. Or you're doing routes in strip malls where a lot of the meters were buried, and there's water in the meter enclosure so sometimes you need to find a way to bail the water out. I hated that.

Nevertheless, supervisors at Entex liked my work ethic and wanted to groom me for management. They took me to a couple of company picnics, hoping to persuade me to accept a management track job opportunity. They even offered to pay for my tuition if I majored in business. It sounded like an offer I couldn't refuse, but there was something they did not know.

The offer was presented to me less than a week after I had surrendered to the ministry. As I weighed the proposal and thought about the unlikely situation I was in, a feeling came over me. I felt like it wasn't just a potential career move, it was the devil tempting me.

There had been several times in my life when I was sitting in the back pew with the other youth at church and getting convicted with the invitation. I was always that guy who could kill the moment with a joke, do something to make it funny. I recall at least three times, from ages 12 to 16, where I really felt God was wanting me to make a commitment. Each time I was able to slough it off.

Not this time. I knew I was at a spiritual turning point. It was time to decide, what am I going to do with my life? I could take the offer before me, make money, and probably have a good life. I was confident that I could pursue any number of different opportunities and do just fine. But I felt an undeniable spiritual tug, and I realized that all these things had brought me to this moment. God had closed out the book selling path. And now I was no longer in Louisiana and away from all my family. I was alone in this big city, and I needed to decide what I was going to do.

One evening, lying on the mattress on the floor in my apartment, I had a definitive realization. I felt that God communicated to me, 'You need to commit a hundred percent. But if you don't, I will never bother you again.'

That broke me. I thought, 'Okay, you're no longer a kid, you're a man, and you need to decide. Are you going to fish or cut bait here? Are you going to follow the Lord? Because if you say 'no' this time, He's not going to mess with you anymore. He will let you do your thing.'

This time I responded without hesitation.

'Okay, God,' I said, 'you know I'm very flawed, but if you can use me, here I am, but show me the way.' And with that, I started a walk of faith that would become a lifetime commitment.

The next day I called Jane, my future wife, and I told her the good news. She was not happy. She had spent her whole life in a fishbowl as the pastor's daughter and could not wait to have her freedom. And now, I'm doing what?

But I was committed to my decision. Jane and I continued to date, and we talked about it for a couple months. I said, 'Look, I'm going to be on a walk of faith the rest of my life. If God says, 'Go to Africa,' I'm going to Africa. If God says, 'Do whatever,' I'm going to do it. What I need is someone with me who says, 'Wherever He tells you to go, I'm going and we're going."

I said, 'If you can't do that, I totally get it. But if I feel the call, then the only response is, 'When do we go?"

It was a big ask. Jane had to work through that, and she did, though it was not easy because her parents were not into it. They were small town people, Louisianans, and couldn't understand why one day I would go to Kentucky and take their grandkids away. Later, moving my family to California was the craziest thing they'd ever heard. I thought it especially ironic that Jane's father, a pastor, did not understand why I was doing it.

But the Great Commission was in my DNA, and this was a watershed event in my life. And while I could not see the future, I was able to recognize, in the moment, what was happening. That ability helped me cope with a variety of situations, such as the failure of my second year selling books. I understood why I needed to go through that, because had I succeeded again, I probably would have continued a certain path and for God's reasons that door needed to close.

In Houston, I was doing well with Entex; barely two months into the job and they're offering me a management track. But after experiencing my spiritual moment of truth, I fend it off.

Still, I knew I was where I needed to be. At that point I'm like, 'Okay, I like Houston!'

Chapter 5

Back to School with a Little Help from Some 'Angels'

Life in the big city suited me. I also needed to get back to college, so I opened the Yellow Pages, and I found a listing for 'University of Houston.' I called the admissions office and said, 'I'm Ron Ellis. I'm from Louisiana and I'm looking to enroll.'

"Well," they said, "you're going to have to pay out of state tuition."

I didn't know what that was. They told me it involved a big number, and it seemed they were being dismissive. I said, 'Okay, fine' and I hung up.

In the Yellow Pages, not far from the listing for University of Houston, was one for Houston Baptist University. I had never heard of it, but I decided to check it out. I told my boss what I was doing, and he gave me a fast route that I finished quickly so I could get to HBU during business hours.

My apartment was 20 miles in the other direction, so I headed to the campus in my work clothes -- combat boots from my ROTC days, blue Dickies work pants, and a uniform shirt emblazoned with the Entex company name. October is hot and sticky in Houston, so after completing even an abbreviated meter route I was ripe with sweat and dirt.

At HBU, I found the reception area for the admissions and registrar's offices. I walked in unannounced, and Jerry Ford came from his office to help me at the counter. We talked for a while, and he asked me some questions. Ford was a big guy, probably 6'2" tall, and I learned he was from Plainview, Louisiana, which is even more rural than Hornbeck and about eight miles away. We connected at once. I told him that I had surrendered to the ministry, I was single, and I needed a dormitory bed and a meal ticket.

"We don't have anything here," Ford told me, "But why don't you go back and talk to Kenny Rogers?"

The man Jerry Ford sent me to see in the financial aid office looked nothing like the namesake singer and songwriter who, coincidentally, was a native Houstonian. Rather, HBU's Kenny Rogers was short, balding, and sported a Western shirt, brown denim jeans, and an impressive handlebar moustache.

He invited me to sit down, but I politely declined to keep from dirtying the upholstered furniture. So, we stood as I told him my story and what I wanted to do.

When I finished, Kenny pushed a pink phone message across his desk to me and said, "Look at this." As I scanned the name, phone number, and address on the note, he said, "This lady called about 10 minutes ago. She lives in River Oaks. You know where that is?"

I said I did not, and he asked, "Don't you read meters?"

"Yes sir," I replied, "but River Oaks is on Houston Natural Gas. I read for Entex."

At the time, roughly half of Houston was served by one gas system, and the other half by another. I had no idea where River Oaks was.

Kenny laughed and said, "Well, it's not very far from here. The houses are pretty nice in that neighborhood. Why don't you call and ask if you can go see her? She's looking for a Christian male presence to be around the house. I think you might fit the job description."

I don't think Kenny expected anything to come of it, but I made the call and the lady who answered said, "Come on out."

It took me about 15 minutes to drive along the freeway to Kirby Drive and arrive at the luxurious neighborhood known for its stately mansions and leafy namesake trees. The area is home to the exclusive River Oaks Country Club and big-name residents such as James Baker, who served as U.S. Secretary of State under President Ronald Reagan and Secretary of the Treasury in the administration of President George H. W. Bush.

Imagine, this was the Beverly Hills of Houston, and I had never heard of it!

Driving my little beat-up Volkswagen bug, I found the address from the phone message, parked out front, and still as 'ripe' as could be, I walked up the long front yard toward the imposing, three-story house. As I approached the house, the neighborhood security patrol drove by slowly, eyeing me as if questioning, 'What are you doing here and why are you going to the front door?"

I rang the doorbell, and a voice spoke to me from beyond the wall. It was the homeowner, Mrs. Ida Pearle Oberg, who quizzed me briefly via the intercom from within her estate's safe confines.

"Where did you go to high school?" she asked. "Where are you living now?"

After five or six such basic questions, she was finished. "I'll be in touch," she said, never asking me if I had any questions. She asked how to reach me, and I gave her my home phone number. I explained that I worked all day, and I would only be able to take a call early in the morning or in the evening.

One evening not long after that, Mrs. Oberg phoned and said, simply, "I checked you out. You can move in."

The Oberg residence featured a servants' quarters situated behind the house. It was the size of a dorm room. It reminded me of a monastic cell. Directly inside the entrance door was a closet, and to the left was a bathroom with a sink, toilet, and clawfoot bathtub. The small main room to the right had a single bed, an inexpensive three-level bookshelf, a desk with a small lamp and a chair, and an intercom. There was a small, dorm-sized refrigerator for my use, but it was in the garage.

Two or three times a week my intercom would come on and Mrs. Oberg would say, "Would you like to come up?" I tried to always say yes. I would enter the house and go up to the second floor. She had a nice little TV room where we watched mostly Public TV programs like symphonies and the Boston Pops, things I had never been exposed to as a child. At 70, Mrs. Oberg was very small but also very spry.

Stanford and Ida Pearle Oberg

She sat cross-legged on the floor, and she was always organizing something or looking at investments as we carried on a conversation. She couldn't just watch TV. Through those visits, we got to know each other well.

Before long, she started taking me places and I would drive her Mercedes. I had one suit to my name, a green outfit that I'd graduated high school in, resplendent with a green shirt, green tie, the whole nine yards.

We went to places she used to visit with her late husband, Stanford, an Army veteran of World War I. He was an engineer and helped build the Baytown Exxon Refinery, then stayed on when it began operations in 1920. Stanford's first wife passed away, and sometime later he married Ida Pearle, who had been his children's music teacher.

Mrs. Oberg told me that she and Stanford had invested in the stock market. They favored blue chip industries like gas and electric utilities that typically yielded stable, consistent dividends and had less price volatility than many other equities. We didn't talk much about it, but I remember she was a big fan of the dividends that helped fund her River Oaks lifestyle. That was instructive for me, since I was from a lower middle-class family; not that cultured, just good country people.

Because she did not like me coming back dirty after work at my job with Entex, Mrs. Oberg recommended me for a new job at the Briar Club, where she was a member. I worked about 30 hours a week, surrounded by wealthy people. I quickly learned that they're like the rest of us. It's not any value judgment on them, but there are nice ones and not so nice ones; they just have more money.

My duties included booking the swimming pool, weddings, the ballroom, and card tables for the ladies' bridge games. If anything needed to be booked at the Briar Club, I booked it.

Lunch at the Briar Club was always an over-the-top buffet. At lunchtime, I collected tickets when members (mainly middle-aged and older men) came in. Often, there were groups of eight or 10 club members and their guests from some of the dozens of oil companies based in Houston. I calculated the tab by multiplying the number of diners in the group by whatever the rate was, then the member would sign it, and I would drop it into a little basket. After lunch, I delivered the tickets to the accounting office.

That was my job; it was not hard, but I had to wear a suit. I wore my signature green suit every day that I worked.

When the members' lunch service ended, it was lunchtime for the 'help.' That included the bartender, the chefs and servers, the pool guy, the grounds people, and me; everybody who worked at the club was welcome to eat as much as they could hold. So, that's what we did. I learned to really enjoy lunch. We would just pig out, and it was fantastic! But if you took one morsel of food off the premises, you would be fired.

When I enrolled at Houston Baptist University, the Briar Club management was very good about working around my college schedule for me. That worked out nicely. I jam-packed my classes on Tuesdays and Thursdays, starting at 8 o'clock in the morning. I would finish my classes by midday and be to work at noon.

I worked a lot. Mondays, Wednesdays, and Fridays I was on the job at 7:30 in the morning and, typically, I worked till four in the afternoon. Often, I worked on Saturday as well, which helped me clock up to 30 hours a week on top of my class schedule.

I took course overloads at Houston Baptist and achieved some of the highest GPAs of my entire college career. Because I needed to be very disciplined in my studies, I was pretty much a monk, an apt description given my spartan lodgings where I mostly studied and slept. I was working 30 hours a week, going to school, taking overloads. That's what I did, and I enjoyed it!

Plus, I was living rent-free with hardly any expenses, so I managed to squirrel away much of my earnings from the Briar Club.

Before moving to Houston, I had never been to the symphony. Thanks to Mrs. Oberg's patronage, that changed. We would dress up for an evening out (yet another use for that lone, green suit!) and go to the symphony or to the ballet. Afterward, we would go to a nice restaurant and talk into the night over dinner, reviewing and evaluating what we had seen. The way she would critique performances was impressive to me. Rather than negative or fault-finding, her assessments examined the significance and quality of the productions we attended.

Prior to meeting Mrs. Oberg, I was unacquainted with such genteel culture. But these occasions with this special 'angel', as I came to appreciate her, taught me many social refinements including proper dining etiquette. Yes, I was now a college sophomore, but just being around Ida Pearle Oberg was an education on a 'whole nother level!'

Chapter 6

Marriage, College, and Calling

I finished high school a year early and by age 19 I was a junior at Houston Baptist University. I had been dating my high school sweetheart, Jane Dowden, for nearly three years.

Ron and Jane Ellis at the Dowden residence in Hornbeck, Louisiana

The last couple of summers before she graduated from high school in Louisiana, Jane stayed with her grandparents in Houston and worked at Weingarten's, a local supermarket chain. That made it easier for us to see each other, but even then, I was working at another Weingarten's store about 25 miles away and closer to my classes at HBU. Neither of us cared for the long-distance aspect of our relationship, so we decided to get married as soon as she turned 18.

Jane graduated from Hornbeck High School in May 1975. On August 30, six days after her 18th birthday, Jane's father, our pastor, performed our wedding ceremony.

We could not live in my tiny place at Mrs. Oberg's, so for the first couple of months after the wedding we stayed at Jane's grandparents' home. Conveniently, they were enjoying the summer at their lake place at Toledo Bend reservoir on the Texas-Louisiana border. When they returned to Houston, Jane and I leased a small, one-bedroom unit at the Commodore Apartments near the HBU campus, where Jane enrolled and started college that fall.

So, there we were, newlyweds and full-time students, with me working multiple jobs to make ends meet. I worked part-time at Weingarten's and served as youth director at Central Baptist Church in Baytown, about 40 miles away. Life was good.

On Saturdays, I worked all day at the church, visiting throughout the community, promoting the bus ministry, and running the church gym, among other duties. Jane and I would stay overnight in a tiny camper that a kind, older couple from the church towed behind their vehicle when traveling and kept in their driveway at home. I don't know if it was even eight feet long; you could barely lay down in it! I especially remember that showering in the cramped little camper was a challenge, too. But it was the right price, so that's where we would spend Saturday night.

Located on the church property was a house that was used by missionaries while they were home on furlough. Less than a year after Jane and I were married, the latest missionary occupants moved out of the house, and it became available. At the same time, the lease on our apartment in Houston was coming up for renewal. When the church offered us use of the missionary house rent-free, the price was right, and we gladly accepted.

We moved to Baytown and Jane transferred to Lee College. Meanwhile, I commuted to Houston Baptist University to complete my degree.

That Christmas, visiting family in Hornbeck, I sat in the front porch swing at my parents' house. Daddy was in a rocking chair. Such occasions were some of the best times of my life. My father was well educated and a serious, objective thinker. One of the things I most appreciate about him is that he never really told me what to do. Rather, he would ask me a series of questions that would lead me to an answer. We talked for long periods of time, and I loved bringing stuff up and getting this kind of advice because it never felt like he was forcing me to do anything.

I think my father enjoyed it because I was ambitious and always exploring different things. Through the years, I ruled out a lot of things I had been considering because he was so honest and candid in our discussions.

I expected to graduate from Houston Baptist in about a year and a half. After that, my plan was to earn a graduate degree at Southwestern Baptist Theological Seminary, where Jane's father had gone. Southwestern was where you would go if you were in Texas.

As youth director at Central Baptist Church in Baytown, I was gaining a lot of experience with the children's church and bus ministry. But I rarely was given the opportunity to preach in 'big church', and I really felt I was ready to do that.

My idea was to go through seminary while pastoring a small church in the Fort Worth area. Jane would continue to pursue a bachelor's degree in education; the key was me getting a job as pastor in a small church somewhere. That's what I was banking on.

As we talked about my plan there on the front porch, my dad asked me, "Have you ever thought about getting a teaching certificate to have something to fall back on?"

'No,' I said. 'Why?'

"Well, you know," he began in his typically thoughtful manner, "teaching is a really good job to have. You get summers off, and a lot of places need teachers. You probably won't have any trouble getting a job." He suggested I should find out how many added credit hours would be needed, to see if it was worth changing majors at this stage in my program.

"Okay," I agreed. I was good at that stuff.

Once again, the tactful guidance of my father helped me to reconsider an idea in an entirely different light. Looking back in later years, I would see this conversation as perhaps the first step in a significant change of direction, one that would dramatically alter the course of my ministry and life for decades to come.

When I returned to Houston after Christmas, I followed my dad's advice. I was pleased to learn that changing my major to get a teaching certificate would not be prohibitive after all. Besides, I thought, 'If I'm going to go to seminary, I don't need to continue to major in Christian Studies here, and then go up there and do the same thing.'

I had already registered for my spring courses in the Christian Studies program, so I would need to adjust my schedule. But if I changed right away, it would add only three or four hours to my degree program.

So, I changed my major and wound up earning a double major in social studies and education instead. Everybody at Houston Baptist had a double major so it was baked into the curriculum.

Early the next year, Brother Dowden went with me to Fort Worth to visit with Dr. H.L. Drumwright, Jr. at Southwestern Seminary. A former pastor, Drumwright served on the New Testament faculty at Southwestern and was dean of the School of Theology for seven years. I will never forget the meeting.

We arrived and exchanged pleasantries, then Dr. Drumwright sat behind his desk with Brother Dowden and me seated on the other side. After bantering briefly with my father-in-law, Dr. Drumwright turned to me and asked, "Well, young man, what can we do for you?"

I told him about my background, my calling to full-time Christian ministry, and my plan to enroll at Southwestern Seminary.

'What I really need,' I said, 'is a small rural church to pastor in the general area of Fort Worth.'

He said, "Son, let me tell you what it's like around here." The picture he painted was not promising. Dr. Drumwright explained there were thousands of ordained Baptist ministers attending the seminary, all looking for a church to serve. In addition, there were many graduates, some of whom did not want to go anywhere else, looking for pastorates in the area.

"To be frank with you, son," Drumwright concluded, "it'll be a year and a half before I'll refer you out."

Others might have reacted differently when receiving such an unfavorable forecast. To me, however, it felt like a burden was lifted from my shoulders. I had experienced doors closing in my life before. And while this was not the same feeling I had when my second year selling books didn't work out, I was pretty much okay with it. Another door was closed and that was all I needed to hear. It was clear to me that this was not where I needed to be, and I was ready to find out what God had for me.

Driving back from Fort Worth, Brother Dowden was astonished by my response to our meeting with Dr. Drumwright. He said I had misunderstood what we learned, but I was already past the idea of getting a seminary degree. I realized, almost instantly, that there were other things I could do.

I was going to graduate with a degree in education, so I talked with my dad again. "If you don't find something around there you can come back here and teach," he said.

I asked the school principal in Hornbeck if any jobs were coming open and learned about a job teaching history and reading at the junior high school. That worked, so they penciled me in for the position. After I graduated from Houston Baptist University, Jane and I would move back to Hornbeck, and she would finish her degree in education at Northwestern State University.

That summer we moved into a rental house the Dowden's owned

in Hornbeck. While we waited for the new school year to begin, I served a summer internship at the unemployment office where my mother was working. That was enjoyable for two reasons: it was interesting work, and I got paid!

I worked until the end of July, which left some time before my teaching job was to begin in August 1977. Jane and I had a couple of weeks to do something, so we decided to go to Chicago to visit a friend we knew from the military at Fort Polk. We drove Brother Dowden's lime-green Love pickup truck on our journey through broad expanses of open countryside and countless small towns and big cities including St. Louis. It was August 16 when we drove through West Memphis and heard on the radio that Elvis Presley had died.

When we arrived in Chicago, we stayed for several days and saw the sights with our friend serving as our tour guide. We enjoyed the visit, but then it was time to drive home to begin my teaching job.

What I had not realized was that I would not get my first paycheck until October. It was late August, and I hadn't had a paycheck since July. There was no money coming in. I did not get paid in August, but we got through it somehow. In September, there was still no income, and we had no money. When Jane started her classes at Northwestern at the end of August, gas money for the commute became a priority. One of the worst things, I thought, was that not only did teachers get paid just once a month, but their first paycheck did not come until they had worked six weeks. For a lot of first-year teachers, it wasn't like they had quit a job to start teaching and had money to tide them over until a distant payday; many began teaching straight out of college and needed income right away. At least we would be eating with our folks more often until that long-awaited paycheck arrived.

Our families helped in other ways, too. Brother Dowden was sort of a bishop in the area, and almost every Sunday that summer he lined up a church where I could preach. So, I was doing that and receiving an honorarium, which helped with expenses.

That fall, the area's Southern Baptist associational meeting was held at Oak Hill Baptist Church outside of Many, Louisiana. Their pastor had just retired, so Brother Dowden told the deacons that I could come preach for them.

'I sure can,' I chimed in.

Jane went with me the next Sunday when I preached the morning and evening services at Oak Hill. As we were getting in the car to leave that night, the deacons stopped us. Apparently, they had met that afternoon and agreed on a question for me.

"Are you available next Sunday?" one of them asked. I thought, 'Let me check...YES!'

Jane and I made the nearly 20-mile drive from Hornbeck to Oak Hill Baptist Church each of the next several weekends as I continued to serve as 'pulpit supply.' Then, in November, the church called me to become their pastor. We moved out of the rental house that Jane's parents had been letting us use, and into the comfortable three-bedroom brick parsonage at Oak Hill Baptist.

Although my predecessor had served full-time, the church's leaders did not mind that their new pastor was bi-vocational. Along with my pastoral duties at Oak Hill, I continued my public-school teaching job. I was receiving two salaries, and the church was paying me more than I earned teaching school. In addition, the parsonage was provided rent-free as part of my compensation, so we only paid for utilities.

We were doing quite well financially, so we easily managed the transportation needs that came with jobs in two different towns and Jane back in school at Northwestern State. We had a truck and a new Honda motorcycle. I still remember what that CB400F cost, thanks to a *de facto* mnemonic in the selling price: 15, 15, 30. We paid $1,515.30 for a shiny new motorcycle that included two helmets!

Jane loved driving the motorcycle, so in good weather she would ride it nearly 30 miles from the parsonage to her classes at Northwestern State. When the weather was not so good, she carpooled with another lady.

With things going so well for us, it was easy to say yes when we got the opportunity to buy 40 acres in Hornbeck for a tree-farming venture. I thought about possibly using the land for another purpose, specifically to farm catfish. But the acreage was a little too hilly and besides, it was in the wrong part of the state. For any hope of being successful at catfish farming, the land needed to be flatter and closer to a processing plant. Since it was neither, tree farming was an ideal use.

After buying the land, we immediately sold the timber and leased the oil and gas rights. That recouped about 60 percent of the purchase price. We paid off the rest in a couple of years and, in addition to teacher and preacher, I was a tree farmer—all before my 23rd birthday!

That's how we lived for three years. Jane completed her undergraduate degree after two and a half years and began teaching at Hornbeck Elementary School. At that point, we had three salaries, almost no expenses, and we were just throwing money in the bank.

Some people looking at our situation might have thought, "Boy, you guys have it made!" But beneath the surface, I was feeling antsy. At school, people told me, "You need to get on the administrative track so you can be a principal someday." That idea did not make my heart flutter.

Sometimes, people recommended me to a bigger church, but that did not excite me either. By my second year as pastor at Oak Hill Baptist, pulpit committees were coming around to look me over. But the idea of advancing to a bigger church was not appealing. Rather, it prompted me to do a serious gut check.

In a sense, we were sailing right along, so I might have been content with our circumstances and comfortable with the life we were living. Instead, I was feeling increasingly bored. There must be a greater purpose for my life, I thought, but I was unsure about what it could be.

Jerry Ford was the registrar and associate dean at Houston Baptist University, where I had gotten my undergraduate degree. I considered Ford a trusted mentor, so I reached out to him for advice, explaining my situation in a very candid, very personal letter.

'I am pretty good at preaching,' I wrote, 'but I don't wake up in the morning eagerly wondering, what's my next sermon?

'I like teaching, and I've had a fair amount of success at it,' I continued.

'People want to put me on track to become an administrator but again, I don't really want to teach.'

I told Ford I really liked running an organization, but I did not want to be CEO of a business. I loved education, but I did not want to be a professor. I really liked the church, but I did not want to be a pastor. I enjoyed politics, too, but I did not want to be a politician.

'I'm wrestling with the question, where do I land?' I wrote.

I was considering enrolling in the church-state program at Baylor University. I could see myself one day going to Washington, D.C. and fighting for truth with a capital "T."

But I was really wrestling with the call to ministry so, when Jerry Ford responded to my letter, the counsel he gave lifted a huge burden off me.

He wrote, "Ron, you need to back up a little bit. Exhale. Clear your mind and realize this. God created you uniquely to be you. God has a unique plan for you, and that could include being a pastor or not. The main thing is, God wants to use your giftedness, and he wants to use it for the Kingdom."

The impact of Jerry's letter on me was both immediate and enduring. It echos to this day in the statement, "California Baptist University believes each person has been created for a unique purpose." His profound, insightful guidance is reflected even more succinctly in the CBU tagline, "Live Your Purpose."®

The immediate effect of Jerry's advice was that it empowered me to freely consider avenues for Christian service in settings other than the preaching ministry. I had grown up in a rural setting where if one had any spiritual sensitivity or talent, ladies in the church would often say, "You know, you need to be a pastor," or "you need to be a missionary." As if there were four things you can do if you're in the Spirit: be the pastor, minister of music, youth director, or missionary. I heard a lot of that, and it is something that weighs on you.

At 21, I was committed to full-time Christian service and already serving as the spiritual leader of a local congregation. During my pastorate at Oak Hill Baptist, I led a group from the church on a deep-sea fishing trip. We collected and delivered supplies to a rescue mission in New Orleans. We did good things. It was exciting. It seemed like a great situation. Yet I felt bored, and I felt guilty about that.

'There's got to be more,' I thought. 'I can't do this for 40 years.' I was not focused on advancing to a bigger church, nor was I interested in becoming a principal or superintendent of schools.

The program at Baylor was appealing, however, and reading Jerry Ford's sage advice freed me from considering ministry in narrow, traditional terms. Instead, it helped me understand that if I devote my talents to the Lord's work, God will bless that.

The feeling that a burden had been lifted off me was more than liberating; it propelled me forward in a new direction. In time, that newfound freedom would both reveal the greater purpose I was looking for and reaffirm my commitment--since childhood--to serve God and others, whatever it took and wherever it might take me.

Chapter 7

To Baylor and Beyond

The transition from our near-idyllic life in Many, Louisiana to my graduate program at Baylor University in Waco, Texas was purposeful. It was also disruptive, to put it mildly. We gave up two teaching jobs at public schools and my comfortable situation as pastor of Oak Hill Baptist Church, so I could become a Baylor graduate assistant with tuition waived but very low pay. Jane found work at a private Christian school but that, too, paid very little compared to the public-school salaries we had left. That was okay, however, and we quickly adapted to our new surroundings and lifestyle.

For a variety of reasons, however, within six weeks I realized the church-state program was not for me. Considering what we had done to get there, it could have been a devastating discovery. But I had a real sense that God had used that program to get me to Baylor, and without it I would not be there. But I was not there for this program. So, why then? He had yet to reveal this to me.

We became involved in the community and joined First Baptist Church. My Sunday school teacher was Dr. Wilson Manning, a trained psychologist and Associate Dean of Student Services for Baylor University. To be in his Sunday school class, at least one member of a couple had to be a Baylor graduate student. The academic discipline or program they were in did not matter, only that it was at the graduate level. So, we qualified and joined the class.

It was the best Sunday school class we had ever been in, and it was brutal! You had to 'bring it' every week. To get things going, Dr. Manning would sort of throw the ball up and the members would swing away.

The class included men and women who came prepared to display their skills in exegesis. Armed with Hebrew Bibles and Greek New Testaments, they offered sometimes competing interpretations of scripture. In this class, if you ventured an opinion, you had better be able to defend it. That was because, often as not, someone was just waiting to pounce and deftly pick apart your point.

It was great fun and a welcome release for all. It was an eclectic group. Nearly everyone in the class was about the same age, including a Ph.D. student in biology and his wife, neighbors of ours who managed an apartment complex. There were also law school students and MBA candidates that populated our high-powered Sunday school class. It was no place to make a lightweight comment or offer some half-baked idea. As I said, you had to 'bring it!'

Dr. Manning was the perfect guy to orchestrate it all, to throw the ball up in the air and then let us go at it. It was a lively intellectual free-for-all, but at least those in the class weren't hitting each other. When a class session ended, most of us could hardly wait to get back the following week, though some were determined to be better prepared next time. It was a healthy, invigorating environment and the positive fellowship activities we enjoyed helped make it a truly memorable Sunday School class.

The methods I experienced in Dr. Manning's Sunday school class were practical, too. In the years since, I have employed some of them to motivate those I supervise to think and perform at higher levels, with tough skin, and to not be satisfied with just good enough.

At Baylor, I took a graduate-level Christian Ethics course filled with master's and Ph.D. students. The course, taught by Dr. Dan McGee, was another class that helped students develop tougher skin. Throughout my career, I have considered the way Dr. McGee ran that class, and the way Dr. Manning taught his Sunday school class, as profoundly instructive, no pun intended.

When I realized the church-state program I was enrolled in was not for me, I went to talk with Dr. Manning at his office. I told him about what we had given up coming to Baylor, but that after making the move I felt certain that God had something else for me.

"Well, what do you see yourself doing?" he asked.

Since education was a strong part of my background, I said, "I'd love to work at a Christian college someday." But I was not sure exactly what I wanted to do, I added.

Dr. Manning listened as I described my situation, then suggested moving my graduate assistantship from the Church-State program to Education. He introduced me to the Dean of Education, who agreed to the transfer. So, I still had to take a couple of Church-State courses for a minor. But now, my degree would be in Education Administration with a minor in Church-State studies.

As I shifted into the new major, one of my first courses was an internship under Dr. Manning. It involved me shadowing various offices on the Baylor campus. For example, one week I would spend three or four hours in the Development office, where the staff introduced me to various methods used to raise money. Another week, I went to Facilities Management and learned about Baylor's physical plant operations.

At each stop, I asked questions, and the staff explained their processes and procedures. As the session progressed, I learned about admissions and financial aid, how the human relations office worked, and the inner operations of the university's business offices. I realized I was barely skimming the surface of how all the pieces fit together, but it was a fantastic, eye-opening experience. I soaked it all up like a sponge. The more I learned, the more the light bulbs and bells were going off, like a pinball machine racking up the score.

After a few intern sessions, I went to see Dr. Manning to talk about what I was learning and discuss possible next steps. Sitting at his desk, peering through half-rim reading glasses and grading papers, he barely looked up to acknowledge me.

As I sat across the desk from him, without looking up he asked, "So how was it?"

'It's going great,' I replied.

Still looking down, he grunted and restated his question in a different way.

"What do you think about it?" he asked.

'I think it's helped me decide what I'm going to do with the rest of my life,' I declared.

At that point, Dr. Manning looked up. "And what's that?" he asked.

'I think the Lord is calling me to be the president of a Baptist college,' I announced. 'And particularly, I want to go and turn around a struggling Baptist college. And I want to do that, I want to be a president before I'm 40.'

Dr. Manning took his glasses off and said, "What?"

'It's really clear to me,' I said. I explained that in one of my classes I was writing a paper about church-related colleges. One of the main things that was jumping out at me from relevant literature was the projected imminent demise of church-related junior colleges. I even wrote an article about struggling, private, church-related junior colleges that was published in the Baylor Educator. In it, I called them the 'pterodactyls of higher education', a reference to the extinct flying dinosaurs.

I wanted to be a person who could go to a struggling Baptist college and turn it around. I also thought, perhaps opportunistically, that to be a president by the age of 40, I likely would have a better chance of doing so at a struggling college than at one that was managing just fine.

I really wanted to learn how to do that. First, what does a successful college consist of? And second, how do all the engine parts work together? I wanted to understand it the way a mechanic understands a car. How exactly does this work?

In my mind, I began to frame the challenge like the practical difference between laypeople and medical doctors. Most people without medical training look at someone and see that person's facial appearance, skin complexion, hair style, body type, and the clothes they are wearing. A practicing physician is trained to see the person differently. The medical doctor understands that the person has a skeletal system, a nervous system, a muscular system, and a circulatory system. These and many other systems in the individual's body all need to work together effectively to maintain optimal health.

I was fascinated by that kind of perspective. I began to see something similar could be applied to any type of organization including colleges. I realized they all have multiple systems. For example, when you drive by a college you see the buildings, parking areas, and landscaping that make up the campus. That's called the physical plant, and it is one of the first things you see. But you need to understand that the physical plant is only part of the college. There's also a part that involves human elements including the governing board, administrative staff, faculty, students, alumni, donors, and others. Academic programs, athletics, branding, marketing, food service, and auxiliary enterprises are examples of other systems common to most colleges.

Understanding how those systems work and interact, and how different stakeholders perceive them--that's fascinating to me. So, I threw myself into learning as much as I could through that internship. And although I had only a few hours of exposure to each operational area, I gathered a lot of information. Much of what I learned is what I would call executive information. It involved learning the right questions to ask to evaluate a proposal or to solve a problem. So, I approached each session keenly aware that I needed to learn enough about the area to know what the right questions are.

The internship proved especially valuable for me because at the time the Master of Education at Baylor was not designed for higher education. Most of the students in the program wanted to be principals or school administrators, so I was an outlier. But I had great professors who bent over backward for me. Many of them encouraged me to read texts outside their course syllabus. For instance, if the textbook for a course was about school principals, they would tell me, "You need to know these basic concepts, but we think you should read these other books." So, I was doing almost a directed study.

When we wrote papers for our classes, other students were discussing classroom discipline and formulating budgets. I was writing about topics specific to Christian higher education. So, I have nothing but great things to say about those professors who tailored the program for me as much as they could. To use a Southern metaphor, exploring the complex operating systems of a major university through my internship was meat and potatoes. Customizing my course work to study more about what I learned there was pure gravy.

I have always had a bent toward the practical. I sought to thoroughly understand the theories in my course work, but I wanted more than theoretical concepts; I wanted to be able to apply what I was learning in practical ways.

That focus on the practical continued during my conversation with Dr. Manning. I was scheduled to graduate in August, a year after beginning my graduate studies.

He said, "You know, Ron, if you're going to work in higher ed, you'll need to have a terminal degree."

Applying to a doctoral program is usually done in November and it was late January as we were talking. I was already behind schedule, so Dr. Manning suggested that I apply at several places to increase my chances of getting accepted.

I was accepted into Ph.D. programs at both Texas A&M University and the University of Arizona. I considered Arizona for two reasons. First, I would already have degrees from two institutions in Texas. I thought it would be good to get my doctorate in a different region, and I had lived in the West in Las Vegas from age 5 to 13, so I thought Arizona would be a good choice. Second, I was interested in studying under Earl J. McGrath, who produced "Study of Southern Baptist Colleges and Universities, 1976 – 77" for the Education Commission of the Southern Baptist Convention. McGrath had served as U.S. commissioner of education under President Harry S. Truman and President Dwight D. Eisenhower. His study for the SBC Education Commission, the first of its kind, examined basic information that described 49 Baptist-affiliated colleges and universities. I virtually devoured the report and thought studying under McGrath would be a wonderful opportunity.

I received nearly identical offers from Texas A&M, which sent me an acceptance letter, and Arizona, who informed me in a phone call. During that call, I inquired about local employment prospects for Jane.

'My wife is a schoolteacher,' I said. 'What is the situation with the schools there?'

After a long pause, the person on the other end of the phone line replied that the school system had been struggling with finances. It was as if the heavens opened with angels loudly singing, "Don't go this way!"

My choice became clear and soon afterward I declined the Arizona offer in favor of pursuing my doctoral degree at Texas A&M University.

A few months later, I finished my master's program at Baylor. The day I graduated, our families attended the morning commencement ceremony, and we all had lunch together. Afterward, they headed back home to Louisiana. By mid-afternoon, Jane and I were ready for the move to Bryan-College Station, home of Texas A&M University and the next stop on our educational adventure.

We had been renting a furnished apartment in Waco, so there wasn't that much to move. We packed our clothes and precious few other belongings into the back of the truck and headed 90 miles south.

Five days later I started the doctoral program.

My graduate assistantship at A&M required 20 hours a week. While I had to pay tuition, it was just $4.00 per unit with a minimum of $50 per semester for full-time students. And the graduate assistantship paid $600 per month! Still, we were primarily dependent on Jane's salary. We contacted school districts near Bryan-College Station and Jane landed a junior high school teaching job in Hearne, Texas, about 20 miles from the A&M campus. Besides teaching, she also had to coach the girls' basketball, volleyball, and track and field teams.

Jane Ellis posing with a Thomas Jefferson Junior High School women's team she coached after giving birth to her son, Ashton

February 3, 1983

Seventh-grade Demons

Seeing basketball action on the Thomas Jefferson Junior High seventh-grade girls team this season are, front row, from left, Krissy McNutt, Bridget DelBosque, Betsy Shaar, Mitzi Williams, Tracey Erler; back row, coach Jane Ellis, Terry Duenes, Gina Casarez, Debbie Vera, Charline Lott, Asennet Gonzales, Shannon Tindol, Stacy Steenken, Gracie Gonzales and coach Josie Gonzales. The girls are 2-2 in the second half of district play and are 5-7 overall.

(Grady Harrison photo)

Jane Ellis posing with the 7th grade Demons from Thomas Jefferson Junior High School in February 1983

When we married, I was 19 years old. Jane had just turned 18. We agreed that we both should finish our education before starting a family, and for several years we did a good job staying on track.

Now, I was working on my doctorate, nearing completion of my residency, and then Jane became pregnant. The timing was perfect, and we were excited.

I earned 13 units in my first semester of doctoral studies and continued heavy course loads each term for a year. I was pumping it! I completed the nine-month residency and extended it through the summer, earning 40 doctoral units in 12 months.

Texas A&M encourages internships in their programs at all levels. I talked with my lead professor who agreed it would be a good thing to do. I found a posting for an internship at Bee County College in Beeville, Texas. It paid $16,000 for the nine-month school year, which was more than a schoolteacher earned. I applied for the position and corresponded with Dr. Roger Schustereit, vice president of administrative services, about the internship before eventually scheduling an interview. By that point, it seemed all but certain that I was going to get the internship and would be working closely with Schustereit.

During our correspondence, I told him that Jane was a schoolteacher and asked if we could set up some interviews for her during our visit.

"No problem," he replied.

Jane and I went to Beeville and stayed at a hotel the night before our respective interviews. The next morning while I met with Dr. Schustereit at Bee County College, Jane was taken to her interview and shown around Beeville. As expected, before the day was over, Bee County College offered me the internship. Shortly after our return to Bryan, Texas, Jane received an offer to teach at the junior high school and coach all the school's female sports teams.

That fall and winter, the girls' basketball team had a very pregnant coach.

Our first child, Ashton, was born January 16, 1983. Jane remembers putting grades on 149 report cards in the hospital before she and our newborn son were discharged. She took all of five days off after the delivery before returning to work.

Bee County College had opened a beautiful daycare facility about two years earlier, so Ashton was going to campus with me each day for daycare. As it happened, the daycare director was dating my supervisor, Roger Schustereit. In a few months, I would end up performing their wedding ceremony.

When Jane wasn't coaching, she would collect Ashton from daycare after school let out and the two of them would go on home. Other times, I would take him home when my workday ended.

One Saturday, soon after Ashton's birth, Jane had to drive the team bus and coach at a track meet about 30 miles away in Refugio, Texas. They left Beeville at six in the morning and returned home at midnight, with Jane driving both ways. So, there I was on a Saturday, a newly minted, first-time father, caring for our weeks-old baby, alone, for 18 hours. It was a long day for all of us.

The next morning, Jane and I mutually agreed that as long as we had kids at home, she was not going to be coaching any more after finishing her current job.

During my first week at Bee County College the local Southern Baptist associational missionary, whose office was right next to the campus, stopped by to welcome me to Beeville. It was more than purely a social visit.

Ron Ellis in July 1983

"I understand you're an ordained Southern Baptist pastor," he said.

'Well, yes, I am,' I replied, quickly adding, 'We've already joined First Baptist Church, and we're very happy.'

Undeterred, he continued. 'I just want to share with you about the circuit-riding pastors that we have here and the needs of the churches in our area.' He explained that there were a lot of churches in that area--tiny, little churches that all needed a pastor.

'You know, we're very happy,' I repeated to no avail.

"Well, would you go one time?" he pressed on. "I need somebody at Pawnee Baptist Church next Sunday."

I took a deep breath, then asked, 'How far is it?'

The church is about an hour's drive from Beeville, out in the middle of nowhere, he said.

'Okay,' I relented, and that weekend, Jane and I went to Pawnee Baptist Church.

During my doctoral residency at Texas A&M, I was intensely focused on completing my course work and little else. So, it had been a year or longer since I had last preached. Driving home that Sunday after church, Jane noticed I was grinning.

"That felt really good, didn't it?" she asked knowingly.

'It did, to be honest,' I said. 'I really enjoyed it.'

Because I was no longer studying all the time, our situation had changed significantly. My internship was more like going to a regular job where I had time for other things on weekends. I could even study on the job because it was part of my doctoral program. So, it was a whole different ballgame, one without course overloads. A lot of the pressure I had before was off now, opening the door for me to resume bi-vocational ministry.

The associational missionary had gotten positive feedback after my one-off pulpit supply at Pawnee Baptist Church. A couple of weeks later, he paid me a second visit where he presented another preaching opportunity that he wanted me to consider.

"Friendship Baptist Church is about 12 miles out of town," he began. "There's about 20-25 people there, and they've got a little parsonage," he added. "But they haven't had a pastor in quite a while. Sometimes they don't even have services."

This time I was less reluctant and agreed to help. Jane and Ashton went with me on that initial visit to Friendship Baptist Church. We were warmly welcomed by what we soon learned was an interesting group of good, hard-working country folk. Some were farmers, some had cattle operations, and most had deep roots in the region.

That first Sunday, Ashton wasn't just the youngest child at the service, he was the only one there. Since he was barely three months old, some thoughtful church members brought in a crib for him to use. When Jane took Ashton into the women's Sunday school class, however, the crib saw little use. That's because Ashton was passed around from one lady to the next, each one cooing and cuddling the infant visitor. It was a scene that would be repeated every Sunday as long as we were there.

From the start, we could tell they liked us, and the feeling was mutual. So, I wasn't surprised when the deacons approached me after a service and said, "Here's what we were really looking for. We know you're not going to be here long, but we've got this parsonage and nobody's living in it. We'd like you to live there."

The parsonage was very small. It didn't even have a stove or an oven in the kitchen. But it represented rent-free housing as part of the deal they were offering.

"We meet on Sunday mornings, every Sunday," they said. "One Sunday evening a month we have a business meeting that lasts about eight minutes. After that, you would preach about 10 minutes, and then we're gonna eat." They were very clear about how long they wanted that one-Sunday-evening-a-month "sermonette" to last: ten minutes, and no more. Because, then we're eating!

In addition to the Sunday services each week, the church held a workday one Saturday a quarter. Members would come out to clean and repair the church buildings and maintain the grounds. I was happy to accommodate all of their requests and enjoyed a wonderful, if brief, pastoral ministry at Friendship Baptist Church. The people were great, and the church's modest schedule fit nicely with that of my young family.

The experience at Friendship Baptist Church produced many fond and lasting memories among countless others during that formative time. But, like my internship, it too, would end. When the nine-month term at Bee County College concluded, I was hired to continue working month-to-month. Meanwhile, I was already looking for the next step in my quest to become a college president. I had nearly reached the ABD[3] stage in my doctoral degree program at Texas A&M University. I had two highly practical internships at as many institutions under my belt. Now, I was eager to gain more first-hand knowledge and experience in the higher education field.

Searching through job listings in the *Chronicle of Higher Education*, I saw an ad for the position of registrar at Louisiana College. I knew nothing about being a registrar, but here was a mid-level administrative position at a Baptist College and a chance to have my first fulltime job at a Baptist school. I talked with Roger Schustereit, my supervisor/mentor at Bee County College, about the position. He was very supportive, as was the registrar who reported to him, a Harvard graduate who graciously let me observe the workings of her office.

She also gave me a volume often referred to as the bible for registrars, published by the American Association of Collegiate Registrars and Admissions Officers (AACRAO). It's a how-to book, a reference any registrar would keep on the shelf. Just about everything you would want to know concerning college admissions and records is in that book. It covers a broad range of material, from the medieval origins of Western civilization colleges to retention schedules and the development of the Carnegie Unit, which measures the amount of time a student has studied a subject. So, I devoured that AACRAO resource, getting up to speed on the terminology and recommended practices in the field. At the same time, I shadowed the Bee County College registrar and admissions staff, observing their procedures, studying every form they used,

[3] All but dissertation

and picking everybody's brains–all before applying for the Louisiana College job. I wanted to be prepared so I could answer questions on budgets, registration, retention schedules, full-time equivalents--all the things that a college registrar should know.

I also read the catalog thoroughly, even the section in every catalog that most people--including students--skip over, the part with all the academic rules and regulations. I spent a lot of time reading, observing, questioning, and brainstorming different situations so that I understood the system as if I had worked in a registrar's office for a long time. That way, by the time I go to the job interview, I will have far more than the minimum basic knowledge expected of an applicant.

So, that's how I prepared to apply for the Louisiana College registrar's job. It's a technique I would employ again and again in future years as my career path progressed.

Chapter 8

The Louisiana College Years

1983 was an eventful year for Jane and me. Our first child, a son we named Ashton, was born. I completed a paid internship at Bee County College as part of my Ph.D. program. The internship immersed me in higher education administration. It also strengthened my conviction that becoming the president of a college–a Baptist college, to be precise--was my calling and purpose in life.

As my internship was winding down, I applied for a job at a small, private, Baptist-affiliated college in Pineville, Louisiana. Soon afterward, I interviewed for the position successfully and was hired as registrar at Louisiana College (LC).[4]

In my new job, I was responsible for preparing budgets, materials, and facilities for registration of up to 1,000 students. In addition, my responsibilities included compiling, evaluating, verifying, and safekeeping student academic records, among a variety of related duties.

The registrar reported to the vice president of academic affairs, so I interviewed with the president of LC, Dr. Robert L. Lynn. After looking at my background, he told me about a recommendation

[4] In November 2021, Louisiana College was renamed Louisiana Christian University.

that would be voted on at the next annual meeting of the Louisiana Baptist Convention. If passed, it would create a part-time position at the college, coordinator of church and associational relations for Louisiana College.

LC was the only Baptist college in the state. The new coordinator's position would be responsible for representing the college to some 1,250 Southern Baptist congregations, making up 48 regional associations in the Pelican State. The coordinator would be a liaison with the churches, hosting and providing annual training. Also, the coordinator could go into churches to recruit students and ask for funding for scholarships, primarily for LC students from those churches. Finally, the coordinator would report annually to the Louisiana Baptist Convention.

Because of my educational background and pastoral experience, President Lynn said I would be appointed as LC's coordinator of church and associational relations. The duties would make up 20 percent of my workload and complement my work as registrar. I was great with that; it sounded like a fantastic opportunity!

After the recommendation was approved at the state convention meeting, I would often spend weekends speaking at churches throughout Louisiana. I also attended associational pastors' gatherings on Monday mornings, plus the annual meetings of many associations and the Louisiana Baptist Convention. It turned out to be quite a bit more than 20 percent of my workload, but that was fine with me. I loved doing it!

At Louisiana College, I was the person who signed letters notifying students they were on academic probation, or even suspended. There were times that I also conveyed such news to a pastor whose child was in trouble academically. I privately thought about the somewhat humorous situations occasionally created by the two hats I wore at LC. There were times, wearing my registrar's hat, that I would extend a hand to deliver unwelcome news to a pastor. Then, putting on my church relations hat, I would stick out the other hand and ask, 'Would you please consider sending students and money to LC?'

As awkward and uncomfortable as such situations might be, I came to appreciate them collectively as a lesson in leadership. It has served me throughout my career, from that first mid-level administrative position to the Office of the President. Whenever two or more competing tasks require decisive action, conflict may be unavoidable. But rather than looking to avoid conflict in such circumstances, embracing the chaos instead often can lead to creative, even elegant solutions. At the very least, tackling even prickly issues with deliberate, purposeful action to resolve conflict and advance the mission of the organization is the leader's responsibility.

At Louisiana College, the registrar had faculty status, which made me a key member of the curriculum committee. I became steeped in the workings of academics, how new majors are proposed and how they get approved, how and why courses get re-numbered, all the assorted intricacies of post-secondary curriculum. I regularly dealt with the higher education folks in Baton Rouge, the state capital, on such matters, and had a significant role in keeping up with the institution's accreditation.

As registrar, I was a gatekeeper for all things academic at Louisiana College. At the same time, I was the tip of the spear for church relations at LC. Observing that setting through two such distinctive lenses, I began to notice a disconnect between how faculty viewed things and the rumblings I would sometimes hear from pastors about the Baptist college they supported. Seeing and experiencing this disparity in perceptions was at once helpful to me in my dual-focus job at LC. Moreover, it provided a fresh kickstart for me to get to work on my dissertation, which had been dormant for more than a year after our move to Pineville.

I experienced a serious setback while working on my dissertation proposal when the chair of my dissertation committee left his job to go to another university. I had sent what I thought was a pretty good proposal, only to have it returned all marked up with changes in red ink, like so much blood dripping from cruel wounds on page after page.

Wow! I thought. I was stunned. But I made the changes and sent the revised proposal back in.

Again, he returned my proposal, virtually as bloody as before. At that point I wasn't sure what was going on, but shortly after that I learned that my committee chair was leaving Texas A&M. Now I would have to find a new advisor. That was a real downer, because the departing professor was the only faculty member who had experience with church-related institutions of higher education. Everyone else specialized in public school, or public higher education; there was no one with expertise in faith-based institutions.

Originally, I had planned to do a broad study of Christian higher education, inspired by the "Study of Southern Baptist Colleges and Universities" written by Earl J. McGrath. Hoping to move forward with my study, I chose Dr. Maynard J. Bratlien, professor of educational administration, to be my new dissertation committee chair. A former teacher, principal, and school superintendent from Nebraska, Dr. Bratlien's area of expertise was public education.

The project I envisioned for my dissertation was becoming unwieldy, however, and I could scarcely even get my proposal written. It was just too much to get my head around it all. At that point, Dr. Bratlien offered valuable and liberating advice.

"You know Ron, you only need to move the body of knowledge that much," his hand gesturing to show an inch or two. "You can write your tome for higher ed after you graduate," Dr. Bratlien said. "Right now, you need to move the body of knowledge a little bit, so you need to figure out what that is for you."

That really freed me up. I began considering, 'What is something I can do? I'm working full-time and I have a family,' I thought, 'so what would really be helpful to me and my career, and also to the institution where I'm working?'

Since I was both working internally with the curriculum and the faculty, and also out among the churches, I started looking at image.

I wrote my dissertation on "Institutional Image of Louisiana College as Perceived by Selected Constituencies." In my own research, I discovered a research instrument developed by a Ph.D. candidate in South Dakota. Her dissertation dealt with a similar topic, but it was focused on a public institution. Although my dissertation would involve a private faith-based institution, I decided I wanted to use 16 items from her research instrument. I would customize her form with four more items specifically dealing with perceptions surrounding Louisiana College. So, I reached out for permission to use the tool she had created.

There was no internet back then, so I called her on the telephone. When she answered, I introduced myself and said, "I have read your dissertation."

She sounded both surprised and excited as she asked, "Who are you? You read my dissertation?"

Before I could respond, I heard her shout to someone, "This guy read my dissertation!"

'I'm calling because I'm writing a similar dissertation on institutional image. I want to use your research instrument,' I explained. 'I'm going to cite you, of course, but I'm also going to modify the tool a bit so it will work for a faith-based institution.'

If she had been excited just to receive my call about her dissertation, now she was over the moon!

"Yes, yes, you may use it," she exclaimed after hearing my request.

One of the items I added to the revised questionnaire would have little or no application to most public institutions of higher learning. But the question, "What is the spiritual atmosphere on campus?" would be very important to Louisiana College and to the five specific constituencies I selected for my research. These included prospective students, current students, recent alumni, faculty, and pastors of Southern Baptist churches in the state.

That question was just one of many I explored in my Ph.D. research. But various stakeholders' feelings and the actual "spiritual atmosphere on campus" have remained a sincere concern of mine at the faith-based institutions where I have worked ever since.

At that time, image analysis for organizations was an emerging subfield. It was kind of a new thing for colleges, so I was getting in on it early. It helped me sharply define my Ph.D. research and dissertation as the institutional image of Louisiana College as perceived by specific constituencies. And as a result, institutional image would become an integral, ongoing focus of mine, benefitting each institution I would serve in an executive capacity throughout my career.

Our second son, Erik, was born in 1985, about the mid-point of our time in Pineville.

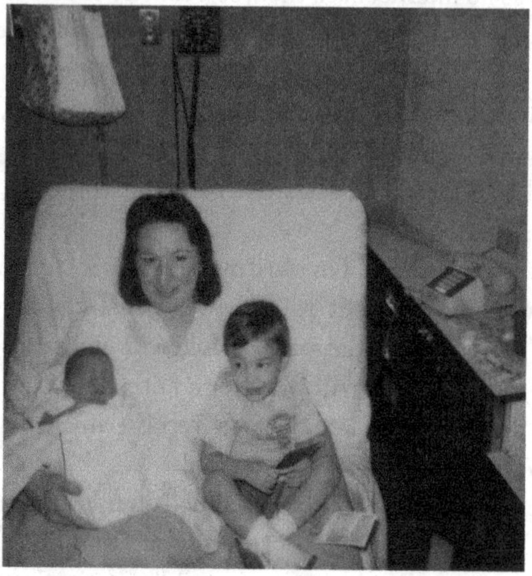

Jane, Ashton and Erik soon after his birth

We now had two preschoolers. Jane was teaching public school at Pineville Elementary. And more than two years into my job as registrar and coordinator of church and associational relations, things were going well for me at Louisiana College.

The clock was ticking, however, and I knew it was time to knuckle down. I needed to complete my doctoral dissertation. I figured it was going to take about a year and a half of intense work to finish. After my personal 'come-to-Jesus' meeting, I had a talk with Jane first, and then with our parents. I told them that until I completed the dissertation, I would need to spend every weekend and vacation singularly dedicated to the task at hand. Consequently, we were going to need help with the kids and some other things. Everyone graciously agreed, and with "Team Ron" lined up behind me, I pushed ahead.

Since the registrar's office was running smoothly on my watch, and because LC was likely to benefit from my research, I secured approval to do some of the work on my dissertation during office hours. That eventually included typing the entire paper by myself on a PC/XT and printing it on the special, blue-lined dissertation paper required by Texas A&M. Happily, by this time, the university allowed the use of endnotes instead of footnotes in theses and dissertations. Previously, footnotes had been almost universally mandated for scholarly writing. But endnotes are much easier to compile, as the word suggests, at the end of the paper rather than on the individual pages such notes explain. That one change was tremendously significant, and one that I welcomed enthusiastically since I did all the typing--and virtually everything else--myself. That included doing the literature review, conducting the survey, performing the analysis of variance, writing the dissertation, and preparing it all to be given to my Ph.D. dissertation committee.

In the days before desktop publishing, just producing a hard copy was hard work. To show how primitive things were then compared to now, computer graphics were still a thing of the future, so I engaged an art student at LC to create the relatively simple line graphs I used to support my research findings.

During my four-plus years at Louisiana College, I was on the team that worked to come up with solutions. I advanced from age 27 to 31, but that was still relatively young to gain experience and exposure to how colleges work at the C-suite level. That was fortunate for me, as it proved to be invaluable preparation for the next steps in my developing career and all that would follow. Soon, I would tick another box, marking the successful completion of my Ph.D., and press on toward my goal of becoming president of a Baptist college by age 40.

Chapter 9

Baylor Redux and Lee College

In June 1987, I was scanning job listings in the *Chronicle of Higher Education*. It was about a week before I would deliver my completed Ph.D. dissertation to Texas A&M University so I could graduate in August. I saw a position advertised in the *Chronicle* for Assistant Director of Institutional Research and Testing at Baylor University. I had a master's degree from Baylor and was weeks away from receiving my doctorate in higher education administration. The job description looked interesting even though the position only required a bachelor's degree. Still, the person I spoke with encouraged me to apply. I told him I would be in the area, delivering my dissertation to A&M.

'It's only 90 miles from Baylor, so I could drop by for an interview,' I offered.

"Sure," he agreed, "that would be great."

I interviewed with several people at the campus in Waco, including Dr. Tom Bohannan, who ran Baylor's recently combined offices of institutional research and testing. His supervisor was Dr. James Netherton, vice president and executive assistant to Dr. Herbert Reynolds, Baylor's president.

My interview with Dr. Bohannan went well, so he took me to

see Dr. Netherton. He skimmed my resume, and after we chatted for three or four minutes, he looked at me and said, "You don't need this job, do you?"

"No, sir, I really don't," I replied. I had a job that I liked, and it was going well. The position I was interviewing for required a bachelor's degree and I had just finished my doctorate. I explained that I felt it was time for me to move on after several good years at Louisiana College. Also, I had earned a graduate degree at Baylor, and I knew the school, so this seemed like a good opportunity.

Dr. Netherton smiled and I smiled; we both knew this job would be a steppingstone, leading me somewhere else. I finished my interviews and returned to Pineville, not sure when I would hear from Baylor.

In mid-August, I graduated from Texas A&M. I was still serving as registrar and coordinator for church and associational relations at Louisiana College. Jane had a job teaching at Pineville Elementary School, and we were both 100 percent in on starting the semester. Then, about the last week of August, I received a phone call from Dr. Tom Bohannon at Baylor University.

"I want to offer you the job," he said. "When would you like to start?"

'June,' I replied, meaning the end of the school year that had just started.

"No, it's got to be sooner than that," Bohannan said.

'Well, how about January?' I asked, hoping at least to get through the semester.

"No," he said again, adding with a degree of finality, "December first is the longest I'm going to wait."

'Well, then, let's make it December first,' I agreed. The timing was less than ideal, but it would give us a few months to list our house for sale and wrap things up in Pineville.

We moved over the Thanksgiving break, and I started my new job at Baylor on December first. Jane landed a job teaching at a public school in Waco. We enrolled Ashton and Erik in a preschool academy and settled into the comfortable duplex we had rented in

Woodway, a suburb of Waco. We became reacquainted with the area and joined First Woodway Baptist Church. Everything was good.

My office was at one end of the fourth floor of historic Pat Neff Hall, the primary administration building at Baylor. The workplace featured a window that reminded me of a porthole on a ship. The windowsill seemed to be a popular resting spot for pigeons that would perch there every day. Their arrival sometimes caught my attention as I stared at the computer screen on my desk. And even after the pigeons had flown off, unpleasant evidence of their visits usually remained.

The Baylor testing office managed the annual American Council on Education Freshman Survey. The survey is a longitudinal look at the experiences, attitudes, and behaviors of incoming college students. It helps colleges track changes in the students they serve. My duties included breaking down the findings of the survey and presenting them to the university's deans and other administrators.

We also conducted major field achievement tests that measured critical knowledge and understanding obtained by students in an academic field. My job was to explain the tests and the benefits of using the results to improve instruction and benchmark with peer institutions. Once adopted, I would supervise the testing process.

I was totally comfortable with that part of the job, and those interactions helped me discover that there were a lot of talented people working at Baylor. It was a great place to work, too, but I realized that I was a cog in a big machine. I would be given plenty of resources to do whatever I was asked to do. However, I sensed there was an unspoken rule that I was not there to knock the lights out; I should just do really good work.

Having such a strong and capable talent pool at Baylor served the institution well. But the prospects appeared dim for me to make the significant advancement that would be needed to achieve my personal career goals. I might be able to make VP when I'm 70, I thought wryly, because people don't leave Baylor. Before long, I grew restless. I needed to move on, so I started looking around.

Dr. Netherton's "steppingstone" prediction was about to be realized.

In the *Chronicle of Higher Education*, I saw an opening for executive assistant to the president at Lee College, in Baytown, Texas. Jane and I were familiar with the school because she had gotten her associate degree there while I was finishing my undergraduate degree at Houston Baptist University.

I was intrigued that a woman, Dr. Vivian Blevins, was the president of Lee College.

Former Lee College dean Walter Rundell greets Dr. Vivian Blevins, new Lee College president in 1986
Photograph by Lee College

I applied for the position. My goal was to get an interview. I told Jane, 'If I get an interview, I'm taking you out for a steak dinner.' It turned out the bar was higher than I had imagined. I later learned that even with a doctorate required for the job, nearly 280 people had submitted applications. It was an attractive position, so when I was invited to interview, I thought, 'I've won!'

Lee College flew me to Baytown for the interview and flew me back home the same day. Dr. Blevins was seated in a nice chair for our meeting, while I sat on a couch, slowly sinking into the soft seat cushion. I don't think this was by accident. Dr. Blevins was prepared with a legal pad and several pages of questions. The first was, "What interests you about this position?" Decades later, this is a question that I ask almost every job applicant that I interview, and at California Baptist University I interview every person who gets hired as a fulltime employee.

I was prepared for Dr. Blevins' opening question.

'Well, my goal is to be the president of a struggling Baptist college by the time I'm 40,' I began. 'I was able to get my Ph.D. in higher education administration from Texas A&M, so I have a lot of theory. I've been putting myself in difficult positions and I would like to have somebody mentor me at the presidential level. I want to learn and take on the tough jobs and be exposed to as much of that as I can, as fast as I can,' I continued. 'So, my learning curve is very steep because I'm on a very fast track.'

Dr. Blevins placed the cap on her pen and closed the legal pad that had been resting on her knees. Without looking, she put them both to the side and said, "Really? I've been looking to mentor somebody."

From that moment, our visit could best be described as simpatico. Dr. Blevins was looking for somebody like me to mentor, and I was somebody who needed a mentor like her. What suddenly felt more like a conversation than a job interview continued for nearly an hour and a half. I thought I had won just by getting the interview. Then, once again, my interview won the job.

Dr. Blevins was an aggressive public figure in Baytown, a city of 70,000 on the Houston Ship Channel. The area was home to the Exxon Refinery, for decades the largest in the world. The U.S. Steel Corporation Texas Works plant, a fixture in Baytown for years, recently had been idled and eventually would be shuttered. Still, Baytown was largely run by blue-collar men, a fact that often created challenges for Dr. Blevins. Because she was seen as a feminist leader, she needed someone who could be a liaison for her and Lee College. That became an important part of what I did.

On one occasion, she sent me as the Lee College representative to an economic development meeting. Also attending the meeting were some very traditional business leaders who had few, if any, nice things to say about Dr. Blevins. I reminded them that the meeting was not about individuals; rather, it was about economic development for Baytown, and how Lee College could help.

I experienced a lot of things for the first time at Lee College. It was like drinking from a proverbial fire hose. That kind of involvement would prove instrumental in my development for the executive level of higher education administration.

On average, there are 22 workdays in a month. I calculated that Dr. Blevins spent about eight days a month in the office. The rest of the time she was traveling, attending meetings, speaking on panels, fundraising, lobbying, or otherwise representing Lee College.

As the executive assistant to the president, I had no line responsibility. No one reported to me. I functioned more like a chief of staff, although with deans since there were no vice presidents. I quickly became the go-to person for deans needing direction from the president. When Dr. Blevins was out, deans would come to me with issues that they asked me to discuss with the president when she called. I kept a short list in my pocket that I would constantly rearrange. That way, the most important question that needed an answer was always at the top. Then she would call, unannounced.

"She's on the line," the secretary would say. "She wants to talk to you."

I would take the call and start working through my list, furiously writing down as many answers as I could. Almost inevitably, Dr. Blevins would declare, "Well, that's all I've got," and hang up before I had covered everything on the list.

The Lee College Board of Regents was required to meet every month. But in the 14 months I worked there, I recall that we had something like 44 board meetings. They were held in the evenings after a full workday that usually started at 7:30 in the morning. Often, the meetings would last until 11 p.m. To describe many of the meetings as 'a zoo' would be an insult to wild animal parks everywhere. Suffice it to say that I saw more than a little dysfunction, but even that was instructive. I learned a lot working alongside Dr. Blevins and seeing how she related to the board.

The first time I was ever named in a lawsuit was at Lee College. We had about 1,100 students in a program at the Texas Department of Criminal Justice Huntsville Unit. An instructor in the program sued the college after being fired for unauthorized communication with one of the inmates. The lawsuit named me as a defendant along with the president, academic dean, and some others at the college.

Being named in a lawsuit was a new experience, one that shook me up a bit. When I mentioned it to Dr. Blevins, a seasoned veteran of such legal matters, she started laughing. "Well, look who just lost their virginity," she quipped.

Nothing came of the lawsuit, but for me it was another valuable lesson. The first time seeing my name in a legal proceeding was unsettling. I have never really become impassive about it, even after dealing with many more lawsuits through the years. But as I learned firsthand, if you are in a key leadership position, especially in a litigious area, you can expect it is going to happen.

I had arrived at Lee College with a lot of experience involving Southern Baptist pastors and their related organizations. I was well acquainted with curriculum and faculty meetings. I knew about testing and institutional research. I brought to the job a breadth of knowledge, experience, and transferable skills. Now I was working with the college president, volunteering to take on the dirty assignments and handle bad stuff that happens at the executive level. Dr. Blevins was very good at giving me those tasks and including me in meetings where important issues were discussed. Usually, I would sit there quietly absorbing it all and thinking, 'Well, that's an interesting solution,' or sometimes wondering, 'Might one play it a different way?' What was important for me was being, in the words of the smash Broadway musical, *Hamilton*, "in the room where it happened." I realized that to make a meaningful contribution in any endeavor it was crucial to have a seat at the table.

Sitting at the table with Dr. Blevins, figuratively and literally,

I learned a lot of things I would need to be ready for whatever my next career step might be. She included me in fundraising activities. We attended events to nurture relationships with donors, like the time we watched drag races from the comfort of a luxury suite. We went to the Texas State Capitol and lobbied on behalf of the college.

It had been years since anyone purposefully examined policies at Lee College to make sure they conformed with the Texas Education Agency (TEA). Dr. Blevins put me in charge of doing that, and it was laborious work. On rare occasions when I found spare time, I would read policies and compare them to make sure they met state requirements. Then about once every six weeks, I would take an early flight to Austin to review the policies with a TEA staff member. Typically, I would arrive for the appointment with my designated agency representative about 9:30 in the morning. We would review materials I had already sent ahead, working through the policies line by line until about 2 p.m. Then I would get back on the plane and fly home to Baytown. I worked this way for months, making sure everything we were doing now--and had been doing for the last few decades--was in sync with state regulations. Any needed revisions would then go to the Board of Regents, which approved all college policies.

Although I worked at Lee College for only 14 months, nearly everything I was involved with proved extremely beneficial for me. The fast pace and broad-ranging, immersive experiences both enhanced and hastened my preparation for executive leadership. Working for Dr. Blevins was like a post-doctoral fellowship. It strengthened a solid foundation in my career development. And it proved to have been ideal training for my next position, where I would have far more responsibility but in a much more relaxed environment.

I learned about the next position the same way I had found earlier job opportunities that had panned out for me at colleges in Pineville, Louisiana and in Waco and Baytown, Texas. It was advertised in the *Chronicle of Higher Education*.

Chapter 10

EVP of Campbellsville College

The path I followed to become a college president was, in many respects, the trail I blazed to achieve that goal. The trail was both intentional and resolute. It traced my journey as I gained theoretical knowledge and real-world experiences that helped prepare me to live my purpose. The trajectory to a decades-long presidency at California Baptist University was uncommonly swift. It also achieved an extraordinary duration, considering the average tenure of a college president is less than six years.[5] Viewed geographically, however, the path was far from a straight line.

The route from my rural Louisiana origins to urban Southern California was circuitous. When I was five years old, my family moved from Shreveport, Louisiana to Las Vegas, Nevada. Then at age 13, we moved back to Louisiana, to Hornbeck, a town of 400. After I finished high school a year earlier than normal, college and post-graduate studies took me from Natchitoches, Louisiana

[5] Sandler, Michael. "Why It's Arguably the Toughest Time Ever To Be A University President." Accessed September 19, 2024. https://www.forbes.com/sites/michaelsandler/2024/02/29/why-its-arguably-the-toughest-time-ever-to-be-a-university-president/#:~:text=Less%20Time%20On%20The%20Job&text=In%202022%2C%20presidents%20had%20been,and%208.5%20years%20in%202008.

to Houston, Waco, and College Station, Texas. After earning a bachelor's degree at Houston Baptist University, I served a graduate assistantship and earned a master's degree at Baylor University. I served another graduate assistantship at Texas A&M, one of the nation's premier land-grant universities, where I earned a Ph.D. in higher education administration with a minor in industrial engineering (labor relations).

Career steps on my path to the presidency at an institution of higher education arguably were more linear. These included a series of successive stints: three years as a junior high school history teacher in Hornbeck, Louisiana, while also serving as pastor of a rural Southern Baptist church; Registrar and Coordinator of Church and Associational Relations at Louisiana College in Pineville; Assistant Director of Institutional Research and Testing at Baylor University in Waco; and Executive Assistant to the President at Lee College in Baytown, Texas.

Each new position represented a significant step forward in my career development. Each, in order, also was necessary to advance to the next. I firmly believe that I could not have gone directly from the registrar's job at Louisiana College to be executive assistant to the president at Lee College. But my stint at Baylor University, however brief, set me up to land the job as executive assistant to the president. Similarly, I could not have advanced directly from an assistant director position at Baylor to become executive vice president at Campbellsville College. But having worked in the C-suite at Lee College gave me the edge I needed to step up onto the next rung of the ladder.

In just 23 months, after working nearly four and a half years at Louisiana College and completing my Ph.D., I went from being the registrar at LC to the executive vice president at Campbellsville College, with two other jobs in between. Sometimes people ask me, "How long should I stay in a job?" I tell them they are asking the wrong question. The most important issue is not how long you should work in a job before moving on. A far more important question is, "In what direction will the move take you?" To put it more bluntly, try to avoid lateral moves. In my experience, if the move is upward, there is no minimum time needed before accepting an obvious advancement.

The early steps in my own career path can serve as an apt illustration. I started out in middle management at Louisiana College, a small, private school. I went from that job to a mid-management position at Baylor, a much larger private university. My next job was at Lee College, which was a community college. But there, I worked directly for the president. I had no line responsibility at Lee College, but I led the president's office administrative staff. That was a perfect position from which to become an executive vice president. Advancing to EVP, like all the steps before, continued my upward career movement. Making lateral moves usually is not good for advancing a career. If one is making an obvious vertical leap, however, it doesn't matter the length of time in an earlier position. In my career, each new job was a move upward. I've never had anyone question how short I was at any place.

I was 33 years old when I became executive vice president of Campbellsville College in 1989.[6] Serving there until 1994 would prove to be the biggest and most important step in my preparation to be a college president. Dr. Ken Winters had been president at Campbellsville approximately a year when I was hired. Formerly a dean at Murray State University, he had no prior experience in private faith-based higher education. By contrast, I had worked at two other Baptist higher education institutions, serving one as both registrar and coordinator of church relations. I also had been pastor of a Southern Baptist church. And I had previous C-suite experience, working directly with two college presidents. Thus, the experience I brought to the role of EVP significantly raised the bar and complemented Dr. Winters' role as chief executive.

Before my arrival, Dr. Winters had rearranged the administrative structure at Campbellsville College. He reduced the number of vice presidents from five to three, which included adding the executive vice president position that my hiring filled. One vice president was

[6] Campbellsville College was renamed Campbellsville University in 1996.

over academic affairs, which encompassed the faculty and the library. The other vice president handled fundraising exclusively.

From day one, I had 13 direct reports covering everything not included in the scope of the other two vice presidents. Among those reporting to me were two former vice presidents that I now supervised. Having so many staff in so many operational areas under my direct oversight forced me to understand and manage myriad internal working relationships.

My office in the basement of the main administration building, directly below the president's office, was furnished with a desk and a chair. There was also a small round table with four chairs that quickly became my go-to place for solving problems. I held one-on-one meetings weekly with each of my direct reports. When one of them raised a complaint or an issue involving another area, I found it helpful to call in the director of that area who also reported to me. My approach was not to embarrass anybody. But we would work through the matter at hand and when we got up from the table, we had a solution, and we were all in. Often, I was dealing with people who literally were old enough to be my parents. But it was never about who was winning or losing. It was about solving problems. It was about being good stewards of the institution's resources and advancing the mission. It's poor stewardship if we are working against each other. More than that, it is often high risk and almost always counterproductive. So, I focused on bringing people together and finding solutions.

Those interactions were helpful to me since so much of what happened at Campbellsville College was my responsibility. Admissions and financial aid were two of the areas in my portfolio. The business office also reported to me. So, I was responsible for meeting enrollment goals that drove the budget at the start of the academic year, and for balancing the budget at the end of the fiscal year.

During fall registration, invited members of my team would meet around 5:30 p.m. to handle challenging financial aid requests. Someone would present a case, describing the student's situation, the family's expected contribution, and how much financial aid they were requesting. Then we would just brainstorm solutions. My goal was to find a way to say yes and keep them enrolled. It was also a way of helping people make their dreams come true and empowering them to roll up their sleeves and improve their position in life. I felt compelled to help make it work for them financially, providing it also penciled for the college. There's nothing like that feeling you get when you are helping people realize their dreams.

One of the most interesting situations I recall involved a farm family. Because they received payment for their crop basically once a year, they needed to carry a balance on their student's account until almost the end of the school year. That was unusual, since most students are expected to pay up front. I remember asking my team, 'Is this request legit?'

One team member said, "They've done this for years."

I pushed back for clarification. 'So, you're saying we should float these people for the fall and the spring, and at the end of the spring they're going to pay?' I asked.

Almost as one, the team replied, "They're good for it,"

'Then so be it,' I said. 'We'll take an IOU.'

We worked diligently to find answers and tailor solutions like that for individual people. Sometimes the solution would include a job as a student worker. Frequently it meant the student or family would take out a loan. But always, the key to making it work was knowing how much the student actually needed, and not just what they asked for.

Working with Dr. Winters at Campbellsville College was where I learned the technique of having individual weekly meetings with my direct reports. It took all day Tuesday for those 13 meetings. I wanted to be informed of everything, and we were solving problems. Then on Thursdays, Dr. Winters would lead the weekly executive council meeting with his direct reports, the vice presidents. I became so enamored with the process that when I became president, I continued it with my vice presidents–my direct reports. That is what I do on Tuesdays when I am on campus. It is the vice presidents' responsibility to make sure that I am informed and there are no surprises, and that we are going to brainstorm solutions when we meet.

Occasionally, I will say I also want everyone to be involved who might need to know about an issue. So, I say, 'Put that on the executive council agenda.' Even though we probably could answer the question, I want others to chime in and be part of the process because we may not realize how the issue could affect other areas.

One of my main rules for the executive council is that we are here to make the best decisions for the university. Everyone needs to have thick skin, including the president as the moderator. And we're not here to build coalitions, to be nice to this person or that one so he'll vote for my initiative. Our job is to be good stewards of the resources entrusted to us.

I expect each of the VPs to ask tough questions. If they don't, then I'm probably going to encourage them to ask a question; I may even have to model it for them. The idea is to have a robust discussion and explore all the challenges and opportunities and problems that we can think of. Anyone who has a real concern needs to bring it up. That way, when we decide whether we're going to do this or not do it, we fully understand why and we are all supporting it.

I expect the VPs to respect the role of the president but also to hold me to the same standard. There have been times when I walked into a meeting high on an idea that I'd had, and they changed my mind because I hadn't thought it through. After a vigorous discussion, I realized they are right, my idea is not going to work.

Admittedly, there have been a few times that I violated this deliberative process, vainly thinking, 'I just have the right way to do it.' Almost invariably, it doesn't work out.

Once, I was convinced that we could help churches that had a businessperson on their staff by offering them specialized training. Our business school had a program that featured a two-week summer session for a national group that trained people to be church business administrators. I thought we could build on that and create a master's degree, an MBA specifically for church business officers. The more I thought about it, the more I liked the idea. When the concept was presented to the executive council there were a few concerns, but I sort of bulldozed those. I felt strongly that this was something we could do to help churches, so we moved ahead with it. We reduced the costs for the program and worked to make it as convenient as possible. But the program never got any traction and after a couple of years, I had to fold the tent.

Eventually, I put my finger on the failed program's Achilles' heel. I knew from my own public school teaching experience that when a teacher gets more certification, a master's degree, or units beyond a master's, they move up on the salary schedule. A lot of the incentive to earn an advanced degree is to get a pay increase. When you work at a church, however, you might get an 'attaboy' but they're probably not going to pay for your MBA. And it is unlikely that you will recoup the expense of a graduate degree. For these reasons, it's a non-starter. I should have known that. If it came up in the executive council discussions, I discounted it by saying we would offer the MBA to church administrators at a reduced price. But the reality was, without that financial incentive to help drive enrollment, the program simply didn't go.

One evening shortly after arriving at Campbellsville College, Jane and I were at a church potluck dinner. I began looking for two open seats while Jane visited with others in the serving line. I was wearing my Aggie class ring from Texas A&M University, where I had received my doctorate. The ring features a distinctive design without a stone. Most Aggies instantly recognize the ring, and typically respond with a friendly greeting.

I spotted two empty seats near an older couple at the end of a table, so I walked over and asked if the seats were taken.

"No," the man said, and when I said 'Okay, then we're going to sit there,' he smiled and replied, "Gig 'Em!" I returned the traditional Aggie greeting and sat down. Jane soon joined us, and we all enjoyed getting acquainted over dinner. That was our introduction to Allen and Dottie Wayne.

Allen Wayne was a Campbellsville native and a proud 1947 graduate of Texas A&M University. He had flown 53 combat missions during World War II, and 30 more in Korea, reaching the rank of Lieutenant Colonel in the United States Air Force. After retiring from the Air Force in 1964, he briefly taught middle school, then attended San Francisco State University to earn a graduate degree in education administration.

Col. Wayne retired again in 1981 after serving as principal of the Fairfield-Suisun Adult School in Northern California. After that, he and Dottie would split each year between California and Kentucky. They would spend the winter in the milder weather of Fairfield, then in the spring relocate to the farm he had bought and restored just outside of Campbellsville. There they would stay through the summer and fall, vacating the Bluegrass State only after the Campbellsville College football team played its last game of the season. The arrival of wintry temperatures was their annual cue to heed the sage advice attributed to Horace Greeley, and "Go West!"

The Wayne's were a lovely, gracious couple and characteristic of the salt-of-the-earth folks we came to know in Campbellsville and surrounding Taylor County. Only later would I appreciate that Allen also was one of the "angels" described in an earlier chapter.

Chapter 11

The Road to California Baptist University

In February 1994, I had been executive vice president of Campbellsville College for nearly five years. At 38 years old, I knew that my goal of becoming the president of a Baptist college by age 40 was looming ahead in the not-too-distant future.

One Saturday, I was with our sons, Ashton and Erik, in the basement of our house when Jane came downstairs. "There's a guy calling from California," she said.

'Who could it be?' I wondered. I couldn't think of anyone I knew in California, much less why they would be calling on the weekend. But when I got on the phone, I heard a familiar voice on the other end of the line. I knew instantly who it was--even as he said, "Hi, Ron, this is Allen Wayne."

The brief conversation that followed is one I will never forget. Col. Wayne told me he had been a member of the Board of Trustees at California Baptist College in the 1980's.[7]

"I just read where the president has announced his retirement,"

---

[7] California Baptist College was founded in 1950. It was renamed California Baptist University in 1998.

he said. "I would like to recommend you for the position, if you are interested."

I remember replying, 'Well, I'm humbled and honored, but I don't know the first thing about that institution.'

Most Baptist colleges were in states well east of the Continental Divide, predominantly the South and Southwest. But having spent eight years growing up in Las Vegas, Nevada, I was open to exploring the possibility.

Five days later, I received another phone call from California. The caller was Dr. C. B. "Bill" Hogue, executive director of the California Southern Baptist Convention and a member of the search committee for the next president of CBC. He said Col. Wayne had recommended me for the job, and he was calling to confirm my interest and ask for my résumé. We chatted for a while, asking and answering questions about my background and experience, and about the college and Southern Baptist work in the Golden State. I agreed to send the search committee my information. And as the call ended, I began a search of my own--to learn as much as I could about California Baptist College.

Years before, I had worked for Dr. Vivian Blevins at Lee College, a community college in Baytown, Texas. She taught me a technique of collecting information to get ready for an executive position interview. I first used the method when applying for the position of executive vice president at Campbellsville College. Following Dr. Blevins' method, I carried out a lot of research about the college and where it was located. In short order, I learned many things that most people would not know unless they had lived there a long time.

In addition, because my research was so fresh, what I learned was top of mind. Through this process, I discovered that even people who were deeply involved in these things probably had not thought about them as recently and as comprehensively as I had. As a result, I walked into the interview for the EVP position--and later began the job--with an uncommon level of knowledge and immediacy with the information.

Before I interviewed for the EVP position, Dr. Blevins told

me to subscribe to the local newspaper and read up on issues in and around Campbellsville. She instructed me to secure and study Campbellsville College budgets, audits, board minutes, and faculty minutes for the last three years. She told me to obtain and scrutinize the school's most recent self-study. And she said I also needed to familiarize myself with the college catalog and current marketing and fundraising materials. I saw that much of the information she told me to gather would either include or function as key performance indicators. These would be useful for evaluating the college's effectiveness and potential. One item on her list, however, surprised me.

"You need to get a yearbook," she said.

'What would I need a yearbook for?' I asked. Her response was as thorough as the scope and variety of reports and materials she said I needed to assemble.

"You need to get a list of all the people you're going to interview with, because for this position you're going to be there several days and you're going to go from one group to another," Dr. Blevins explained. "So, get the names of all those people and then look through the yearbook and see, are any of their pictures in there?

"Make a photocopy of each one to use as a flashcard. On the back, write down information about that person," she continued. "Put a rubber band around all this, and then review the cards when you are waiting for a plane or sitting in a lobby before a meeting. That way, not only will you be able to recognize people on sight, but you're also going to know several things about them that you glean from sources such as the local newspaper, catalog, and yearbook."

It was a brilliant strategy! I followed the procedure diligently as I interviewed for the position of executive vice president of Campbellsville College. And when I met several of the people for the first time, I instantly recognized them and knew something about them, thanks to the flash cards I had made. It was an effective and powerful technique. Several of those I met were impressed when I called them by name without an introduction or commended them on a recent achievement.

Dr. Blevins' technique of collecting and assimilating detailed information about a job opportunity had served me well. I made good use of it when I applied for and was hired as executive vice president at Campbellsville College. Five years later, I would dust it off and use it again. It had put me in a strong position to succeed before, so I repeated the process as I explored a possible move to California Baptist College. This time, my sights were focused on the next rung up my career-goal ladder–the office of president.

I would spend 150 hours–nearly the equivalent of four, five-day work weeks–researching California Baptist College. I still have a two-page list of materials that I asked the college to send me. A handwritten note on the list shows the items were mailed on March 10, 1994. Among the items I received were a college catalog, faculty-staff handbook, student handbook, audits for the previous three years, the current year's operating budget, and minutes from the faculty, executive council, and board of trustees' meetings. Other items included an application form, financial aid information, admissions materials, viewbook, alumni magazine, development materials, strategic plan, self-study, and accreditation report. I also received copies of the Riverside Press-Enterprise newspaper and a packet of information from the Greater Riverside Chambers of Commerce.

Included in the materials I received was the institutional mission statement articulated in CBC's 1954 Articles of Incorporation. I was intrigued by the statement and studied it closely. It would become foundational for my vision to build a university committed to the Great Commission.

My in-depth research was designed to help me quickly learn about CBC and its Southern California setting. Learning about the college was not enough. I also wanted to know about Riverside, California and the surrounding region known as the Inland Empire. What was their history? Who were the people who lived there? What were their demographic and economic profiles? Where did they fit in the pecking order?

To understand CBC within the context of higher education in

the state, I contacted the California Department of Education in Sacramento. I asked them to send me the most recent annual report on higher education. The volume I received was nearly 300 pages. An important nugget that I took from the report, which I saw as a condition for success, was this: in California, the most populous state with the largest public higher education system in the nation, more than half of all graduate degrees are granted by non-public institutions, and two thirds of all professional degrees such as law and medicine also are granted by non-public institutions. I had worked in higher education in Louisiana, Texas, and Kentucky, and that was not the case in those states. I found this to be one of the most intriguing facts in the report. The potential was amazing.

The more I studied materials related to CBC and maps of the region, the more that potential seemed to increase. I saw there was a good airport, Ontario International, less than 25 miles from the campus. It also looked as though the college could not be more ideally situated for growth. Riverside is 60 miles east of downtown Los Angeles and 90 miles north of San Diego. Population growth projections saw the region eventually filling in the valleys between mountain ranges from Palm Springs to Santa Monica, with Riverside right in the middle.

Years later, those projections were realized. Based on the 2010 Census, the area that included the City of Riverside received a new congressional district. The fact that the campus of California Baptist University was in the new congressional district confirmed its location as ground zero for the explosive growth in the Inland Empire.

I came to understand that in California, virtually everything starts on the coast and moves inland. Wealth, jobs, and political power in the state are concentrated in the coastal regions. These dissipate rapidly as you move east and away from the coast. The coastal counties, particularly the Bay Area, usually get first cut. Then it goes down the coast, and then it moves inland. Inland areas tend to get crumbs, figuratively speaking. Among these areas are Chico, in the north; Fresno and Bakersfield in the Central Valley; and

San Bernardino, Riverside, and the Coachella Valley in Southern California.

Often, areas that are on the short end of the political power stick experience major infrastructure lag time. A common lament of residents and institutions in these areas is that they don't get a fair share of state judges, schools, or roads. That could be seen as a negative, and it is. Conversely, it also could be seen in positive terms as an opportunity. That is because it likely means the state is not going to be putting money into public colleges and universities in the inland regions at the same level as they are doing along the coast. So, if your ministry is to serve the needs of people by way of higher education, as it is for California Baptist University, that creates a tremendous opportunity to build market-sensitive programs. It opens the door for what I call opportunity planning, which I will discuss in a later chapter.

After I had obtained and digested the information, I used it to create a vision for CBC and outline what I would do if I came there. I was not interested in just holding a position; I would be coming here to accomplish a mission. So, during the interview process, I was selling not just myself, but also my vision. I wanted to see, are they going to buy into it? I am interested in doing that, but are they interested in having that done? To be frank, if they're not, then I'm probably not that interested in coming.

In May 1994, three members of the search committee came to Campbellsville for our first in-person interview. They also wanted to speak with my pastor, my current boss, and my wife, Jane, who was teaching at the elementary school. The delegation included John Funk, a businessperson and chair of the CBC Board of Trustees; Rev. Scott Williamson, a trustee and chair of the search committee; and Dr. C. B. "Bill" Hogue, executive director of the California Southern Baptist Convention.

We arranged to meet at a local restaurant, so at the appointed time I was in my car, parked outside, waiting for them. I wondered how I would know when they arrived, but when they did it was instantly clear. If you know anything about a Baptist pulpit committee, they looked just like that. It was obvious that these fellows were not from around there. I greeted them, wryly, as the 'three wise men who came to the East.'

After briefly exchanging pleasantries, we went to the college where the visitors met with President Winters. I remember hearing laughter as I waited outside Dr. Winters' office. Next, I took them to the church a few blocks from campus. They met privately with my pastor while I waited in the reception area with the pastor's administrative assistant. Again, there was an embarrassment of laughter coming from the other side of the closed door. What was supposed to be a 15-minute visit stretched to nearly three times that long. Things seemed to be going well, but we were way behind schedule. Finally, we drove out to see Jane at the very traditional, three-story elementary school building where she was teaching. Evidently, everybody and their brother knew we were coming. As we pulled up out front, people were almost hanging out the windows. There was no secret to what was going on.

The visit by the 'wise men' took place in early May, and everything went exceedingly well. But afterward, I heard nothing from the search committee for weeks.

'If it all works out by the end of June, we could be there by August,' I thought. Day after day, I continued hoping for some signal from the committee, but all I got was radio silence. No communication. Crickets.

I remember telling Jane, 'I think I ought to call out there and just see what's going on. Maybe they need more information.'

"No, it's their move," Jane said. "Let them call."

She was right of course, so we waited. And we waited some more. May ended without any word from the committee. I didn't hear anything in June, either. Before long, it was mid-July.

Much later, I would learn that the lack of contact was because there was no search firm managing the process. College trustees had chosen one of their number to serve as interim president. Jeff Sanders, an insurance executive from Arkansas, was focused on keeping things running at CBC until the new president was hired.

Members of the search committee were simply busy with their regular jobs.

In my role as executive vice president at Campbellsville College, I had a great relationship with the president, Dr. Ken Winters, both personally and professionally. Whenever he was off campus, I would serve as acting president. I worked hand in glove with him on nearly every aspect of college operations and external relations. He and I would meet every week to review all manner of issues and topics. He would bring up any matter he wanted handled, and I would bring up whatever I needed to discuss. Since February, I had been keeping Dr. Winters posted on developments with my candidacy at CBC.

In August, Jane and I would make our second trip to California as a candidate for president, this time for the final interview. It was Tuesday, two days before Jane and I would fly out. I was probably going to be offered the position of president at CBC. During my weekly one-on-one meeting with Dr. Winters, we covered all the college business that needed our attention. He did not have anything else to talk about, and since I had nothing else to discuss, I asked a parting question.

'Do you have any advice for me as we go out to California?'

By nature, Dr. Winters was a mild-mannered, methodical individual. I never really saw him get angry or display much passion about most things. I figured he would respond to my question by offering some sage counsel or, at the very least, kind words of blessing and encouragement. As I sat waiting for his reply, however, his expression suddenly grew very serious. What he told me next still rings in my ears.

Shaking a forefinger for emphasis, Dr. Winters said, "You know, you can be a president at 38, and a former president at 40. And if you are, you'll probably never be president again."

Wow! That was not at all what I had thought he would say. I was expecting to hear, "We're going to be praying for you," or "We're encouraging you."

I have been speechless only a few times in my life. This was one of those times. I do not recall if I said anything in response to Dr.

Winters' stark warning. But silently processing his words seared them in my brain. So much so, that they became a tremendous motivator that would serve to focus my thoughts and efforts for years afterward.

I was taking a very big career risk. I was in a very good situation at Campbellsville College, arguably where I was the heir apparent. My wife had a good teaching job. Our sons were 11 and nine and they were happy in our idealized, Beaver Cleaver kind of environment. By comparison, the situation in California was a study in contrasts. For one thing, it was just different culturally than Kentucky. The school where I was interviewing was struggling just to pay its bills, let alone increase enrollment and achieve sustainability. But when I did 150 hours of research, I learned some things that really attracted me. One was the number of people in the region. There was a perception that people in the Inland Empire did not have as much money or other resources as their coastal counterparts. But compared to rural Kentucky, there were many more people and much greater wealth. Even the disparity in infrastructure writ large presented a powerful opportunity. Along with the deficit in state judgeships per capita, the region where CBC was located also was lacking in doctors, nurses, and hospital beds per capita. I saw those factors as opportunities to minister. Further, the population of the two-county Inland Empire almost equaled the entire state of Kentucky. Most of that was in the western parts of Riverside and San Bernardino Counties. It was the opportunity to service these underserved markets that really attracted me.

From the extensive research I had done, I was able to develop and articulate a turnaround vision for CBC, which was struggling financially and in survival mode. In my final interview with the trustees I said, 'If you agree to this, and I come, we're going to do this. I'm not selling it to the faculty, the donors, or anybody; we're going to implement it because the situation demands it.'

It was a bold assertion and not the kind of thing I would say if things had been more normal. But the college was in dire straits. I felt it was necessary for me to have the ability to put together a plan, explain that plan, and to let them know that if they hired me, I was going to implement the plan. Still, I realized how difficult it was going to be to succeed. The odds were strong that the school might not be around in three years if they did not get the right person to do a turnaround.

After the interview concluded and the trustees were about to vote, I was with Jane in another room. I told her, 'Now they're going to be voting whether to offer us the presidency. This is a risky decision for us,' I said solemnly, and then I put out a proverbial fleece.

'If 10 percent or more of the board do not vote to call us, I'm going to take that as a sign and we're not going to accept,' I said.

Jane, incredulous, looked at me without saying a word.

'I'm serious,' I said.

We were waiting in the historic James Building in a room just down the hall from the Staples Room, where the board was meeting. After the trustees voted, Scott Williamson, the search committee chair, walked in to announce the result.

"Congratulations," he beamed. "You're a new president!"

He put out his hand out to shake mine, and I said, 'Wait, what was the vote?'

Williamson looked surprised. But then, as though I ought to have known already, he said, "Well, it's unanimous."

'Well, then I'll accept it,' I responded.

Williamson escorted us back into the board meeting. We received a standing ovation from trustees as I formally accepted their offer to become the fifth--and youngest--president of California Baptist College.

Student orientation for the fall semester was being held outdoors that day at Harden Square, a grassy courtyard behind the James Building. One of my first activities as president-elect was donning a signature CBC embroidered necktie to be introduced to the new cohort of incoming students.

Jane had started her new school year two weeks earlier, not counting the teacher orientation. The fall semester was already underway at Campbellsville College, where I was executive vice president. It was a very busy time for both of us. Additionally, our boys were in school back home, so it was decided that my start date at CBC would be November 1, 1994. That was fast, giving us barely two months to wind things up in Kentucky and move to Riverside.

When I came to CBC, the board of trustees had given me a mandate to reverse the persistent, unresolved financial stress that had the school teetering on the brink of collapse. Moreover, the board's unanimous vote to hire me as president gave me explicit authority to explain what we were going to do, and then look for the people needed to help get it done. That is an extremely unusual situation in higher education.

I sensed it was the culmination of what I had been preparing for since age 25. I felt that divine guidance had directed each step of the goal-oriented journey that had consumed the past 13 years. It had been a resolute, complex journey that included developing a plan, completing two additional academic degrees, and advancing through a series of jobs, each with more responsibility than the last, on the ladder to my career goal.

I truly felt I was born to do this. And I sensed that the same divine guidance that directed my preparation had now brought me to this place. But without the convergence of two crucial factors, the turnaround opportunity that CBC presented, and the authorization granted by the board of trustees, I might never have reached my goal to become president of a struggling Baptist college by the time I was 40.

I had done it at age 38, becoming one of the youngest college presidents in the United States.

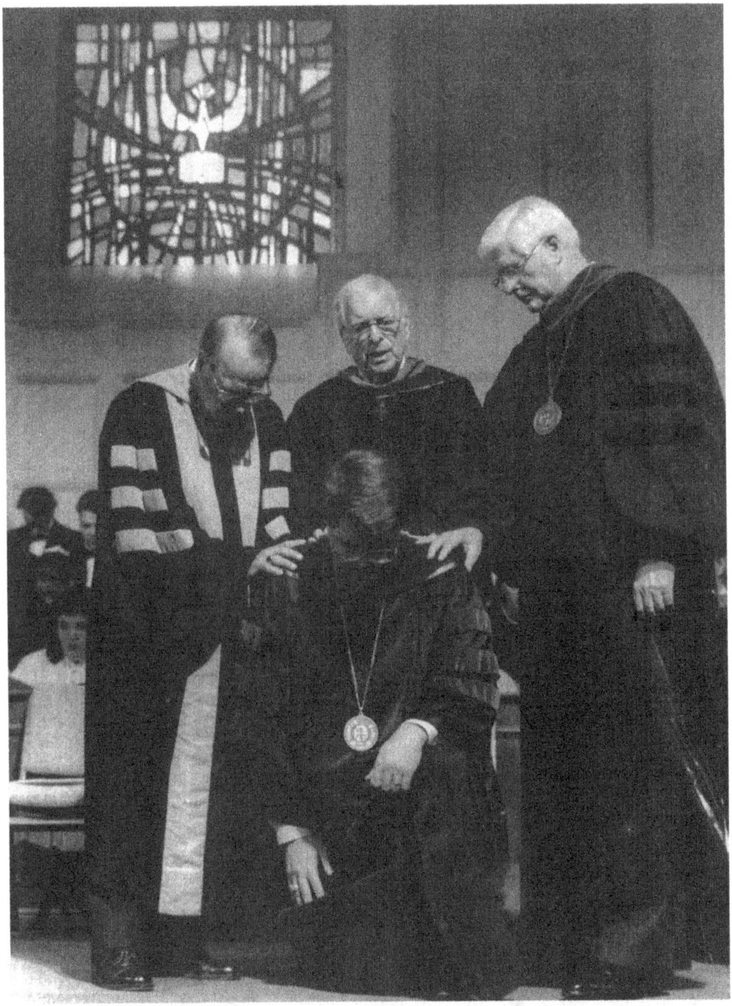

Dr. Ellis kneels during his inauguration ceremony as three of his predecessors pray for God's leadership for him and the college; From left, James Staples, president from 1970-1983; Loyed Simmons, president from 1958-1969; and Russell Tuck, president from 1984-1994

Achieving that momentous first step toward fulfilling what I considered my life's calling had taken years of purposeful academic and professional training, and a lot of hard work.

The Ellis family at California Baptist College

The second part of my goal, turning the struggling school around, was about to begin.

Chapter 12

Casting the Vision for Growth

California Baptist College was founded in 1950 by churches of the Los Angeles Southern Baptist Association. The college opened with 42 students in September 1950 in borrowed facilities at First Southern Baptist Church of El Monte, a city in the San Gabriel Valley east of the City of Los Angeles. One year later, enrollment at the fledgling institution more than doubled to 98 students.

After four years, with enrollment numbering 220 students, CBC had outgrown the space it was using at the church. College trustees and administrators began searching for a permanent campus site, eventually buying property at 8432 Magnolia Avenue in Riverside, California. The site was built as a retirement home for members of the Neighbors of Woodcraft fraternal organization. Construction on the two-story main building began in 1922. It featured 102 large, private residential rooms with wide hallways. More than a century later and after multiple renovations, this historic structure is known as the James Complex. It remains an integral component of the California Baptist University campus, housing classrooms, laboratories, faculty offices, and administrative space.

Another two-story building included in the former Neighbors of Woodcraft site acquisition was also repurposed and has served the university for nearly seven decades. The Neighbors of Woodcraft infirmary, completed in the 1930's, today houses the Annie Gabriel Library at CBU.

California Baptist College bought the Riverside property in late 1954. Over the Christmas break that year, students, faculty, and friends moved books and materials from the El Monte church to the new campus location. Classes resumed at the new site in early 1955, with some of the Neighbors of Woodcraft residents, and even some of the retirement home's livestock, continuing to live on the property. The buildings, while substantial, were not designed for the needs of a growing young college. But there was no money to convert the facilities into classrooms and administrative offices, so they made it work.

From the beginning, the college struggled to make ends meet financially. During the early years, 'Save the College' campaigns became regular recurring events. Every 18 months to two years, some of the founding pastors or other supporters would visit Southern Baptist churches throughout the state. Usually, the visiting preacher would deliver a sermon based on the biblical text, "There is a lad here," from John 6:9. The message appealed for monetary support to keep the college afloat. The offerings collected during the campaigns would basically pay off the college's current accounts. After that, operating deficits would start mounting again.

Insufficient resources prevented CBC from being accredited for more than a decade after its founding. Accreditation of an institution of higher education is important for several reasons. It ensures academic quality and affirms that the school demonstrates positive student outcomes such as retention, graduation, and employment. Students enrolled at accredited schools gain greater access to federal loans and scholarships. Many such programs require that students attend an accredited postsecondary institution to be eligible. Accreditation also helps the transfer of academic credits among accredited institutions.

Among other conditions for accreditation, the regional accrediting agency, WASC, requires a certain count of books in the library. CBC did not meet that condition until 1961. That year, a supporter of the college stepped in to help by donating her personal library to CBC. Her generous act enabled the first significant development of the collection. More importantly, it pushed the college over the top, and WASC granted accreditation to CBC for the first time. California Baptist College memorialized the milestone gift by naming its library after the donor, Miss Annie Gabriel.

Annie Gabriel being recognized at a ceremony during chapel on December 9, 1960

In 1994, the college was 44 years old and still in its historic cycle of need; it just could not quite seem to get over the hump. The school had 297,000 square feet under roof, but there was significant deferred maintenance. I don't think they had ever been able to catch up; there was deferred maintenance when they bought the property, and then it just compounded as time went on.

On the positive side, at least there was room to grow. CBC had structures totaling 297,000 square feet on 59.5 acres, about the area of a large shopping mall. The campus had 75 acres, but in 1991 college officials had sold more than one fifth of the land to keep the doors open. Selling 15.5 acres for $5.2 million basically paid down the bills that were owed and bought some new carpet and other things. When I arrived as president three years later, it appeared the infusion of cash had not solved the underlying financial issues. It reminds me of paying off someone's credit card, and then they're good until they need it paid off again. CBC remained in a financial hole and struggled to dig out.

As I began my presidency on November 1, 1994, the situation at CBC was dire. The school was in survival mode. I had known there were problems before I came; I just did not know how bad things really were. CBC had 870 students enrolled in the fall of 1993. One year later, in the fall of 1994, enrollment had shrunk nearly eight percent to 808. The operating budget was $11.3 million, but I learned the college was facing a projected $834,000 deficit in the current fund. There were only eight months remaining in the fiscal year that would end on the following June 30. The situation was far from rosy. My first order of business was to balance the budget.

Looking at CBC, especially as I started interviewing for the presidency, I began to see that there was a critical mass of people who realized this place is going down. I sensed a shared concern among some board members, faculty, and other employees. From the standpoint of a change agent, this is a necessary condition for success.

The reason many organizations have difficulty changing is because things are perceived to be not bad enough to require change. Fortunately, enough key people at CBC recognized the seriousness of the situation and I was given a chance to turnaround the college's dire financial situation. I worked to identify a core group of change agents, direct and empower them, and protect them from internal obstacles while being cautious to not unnecessarily upset those we needed to teach and serve our current students. The conditions for success must be present to support a reasonable expectation of success. CBC was open to trying new things.

For an organization that needs to change, the first condition is, are they ready? The example I usually give is about helping someone overcome alcoholism. There is not much one can do, unilaterally, to change an alcoholic's behavior. They might say or do anything in order to get the next drink. Often, that is the one thing an alcoholic focuses on, getting the next drink. When things get so bad that the person says, I'm an alcoholic and I need to get better, someone may be able to help them. It often takes a catastrophic event such as a health crisis, or a booze-fueled accident that causes the alcoholic to fear that they are going to die. At that point, you may be able to put them in a twelve-step program. If that happens, then there's a possibility that they will get better if they follow the guidance.

I believe it works much the same way for institutions. The number one condition for success for such an organization is, are there enough people in important positions who realize that the institution needs to change? A second condition for success is the context in which the institution operates. Will stakeholders accept change and, if not acceptance, will there be toleration? Will people tolerate someone coming from outside and making the change?

When I was interviewing, I had painted a picture for the trustees that I would be working for. It was based on 150 hours of research and preparation, which gave me a realistic understanding of the context in which they operated. In multiple interview sessions, I talked about the institutional mission statement contained in the 1954 CBC Articles of Incorporation. I outlined my views about the statement to the search committee and the full board. I said it provided a rationale for expanding academic offerings well beyond the liberal arts. It also supported focusing on the Great Commission at the heart of the institution.

After the trustees hired me, affirming my vision to lead CBC to viability and beyond, I shared that same conviction with the faculty, the staff, the alumni, and the community.

'We are going to transform CBC from a liberal arts college to a university committed to the Great Commission,' I said. I believe Southern Baptists are at our best when we emphasize the instruction Jesus gave his followers in Matthew 28:19-20. When it comes to sharing the gospel around the world, Southern Baptists are united and strong in our conviction.

Accomplishing that transformation would require significant resources, and CBC was in a financial crisis that posed a genuine existential threat. There are multiple ways to erase a budget deficit, including reducing spending and increasing revenue. I knew we had to do both. So, in a town hall meeting with employees soon after I arrived as president, I said we were going to have 1,000 students enrolled the next fall. Boosting enrollment alone would not turn things around, but it would help by increasing revenue.

Another thing I told the faculty at that meeting was that the board had hired me to lead the effort to build a university committed to the Great Commission. When I arrived, CBC had been marketing itself and saw itself as a liberal arts college. So, one of my tasks was to build a university from a liberal arts college. First, I had to explain to people the difference between a liberal arts college and a university. In a liberal arts college, academic power stems from students having to take a professor's courses in order to graduate. It usually means the school's general education (Gen Ed), or core curriculum, continues to grow and become ever more specific. For example, students do not just have to take a political science course; they must take the one I teach, although this would be an extreme example.

That gives the professor a lot of power, not to mention job security. But when that happens, it also tends to hold the school back. A question I often ask people about their college choice is 'Why did you pick that institution?' No one has ever answered, "Well, they didn't have my major, but I just fell in love with their Gen Ed!"

I am not knocking Gen Ed. It is an integral part of an academic program. Students need these classes, usually during the first two years of an undergraduate degree program. General education supplies a needed foundation for the rest of the student's education. But the more flexibility you can provide with that, the better for the students and the institution. We would continue to have liberal arts and Gen Ed courses at CBC, but I knew they were not going to be decisive in attracting the students we needed to increase enrollment.

What drives enrollment at universities are the academic programs they offer. In the town hall meeting, I described the importance of academic programs by using a metaphor I had devised, comparing a flagship with the other vessels in a naval fleet. The term "flagship" comes from the naval tradition of the commanding officer of a fleet of ships flying a distinctive flag to indicate his presence. The ship itself was called the flagship, and was usually the most powerful in some way, such as being larger, better armed, or faster than the other ships.

Over time, the term that dates to the seventeenth century has been used more loosely to describe the best, largest, or most important thing in a group. In my metaphor, an academic program is the flagship, and Gen Ed requirements make up the service program that supports it.

'When a fleet goes out to sea, it's because of the flagship,' I said. 'The fleet's commanding officer, usually an admiral, is on the flagship that carries his flag, and the fleet derives its mission from the flagship's mission.

'But flagships do not go to sea alone; they need support,' I continued. 'They might have battleships, destroyers, cruisers, frigates, and all kinds of other service ships around them. All these vessels are important, but the reason the fleet is going out is because of the mission of the flagship.'

Driving home the metaphor, I said, 'As we transition CBC from a liberal arts college to a university, we're going to have flagship programs and service programs. Here's my definition for each. If more than 50% of the credit hours generated by your area are needed to graduate from here, you're a service program. That's not a bad thing; that's just where you are. On the other hand, if more than half of the credit hours generated by your area are not needed to graduate from here unless you're in that major, minor, or concentration, you're a flagship. Now, I'm going to listen to everybody's ideas and opinions, but I'm going to listen to the deans and the people who are in the flagships more.

'Just to be clear," I added, 'I like to be treated like an adult, and I like to talk to people like an adult. This is an adult operation. So,

I just want to be very clear and communicate with you that that's where we are.'

Programs are the reasons people choose to attend a particular university. One can graduate from our school without taking a business course, a nursing course, or a speech language pathology course. Education, business, nursing, engineering -- they almost exclusively provide courses for students who are majoring or minoring in their programs. Those are flagships, the ones that drive enrollment.

Ask a current or former college student, why did you go there? The answer probably will be something like, "Well, they have a great nursing program." "They have engineering." "They have a speech language pathology program." An important reason people choose a particular university is because it offers the program they want. There are other factors in the decision, but if the school doesn't offer the programs students want, those students probably are not coming.

The town hall meeting was one of many places I shared my vision to transform CBC and promote the ambitious enrollment goal. Still, there didn't seem to be a lot of belief in my projection. It would mean increasing net enrollment by 192 students year-over-year, a surge of nearly 24%. But I felt strongly about the audacious enrollment target. I thought we could even exceed it and enroll as many as 1,200 students. I was confident that at least half of what we were going to try would work. But like a free throw shooter who shoots 50 percent, you don't know which 50 out of 100 shots you're going to make.

Before coming to CBC, I had immersed myself in copious data, not only about the institution but also about the environment. The Inland Empire, composed of Riverside and San Bernardino counties, was home to more than 2.5 million people, greater than 20 states in the union, according to U.S. Census figures.[8] There was a substantial pool of prospective college students. The 1,000-student enrollment goal I had set for the fall of 1995 was bold. I believed

[8] Today, the combined population of Riverside and San Bernardino counties is 4.6 million, larger than 26 states.

it was achievable if we worked smart and hard. Failing to meet the goal was not an option. In the meantime, we needed to get a handle on controlling expenses at the college.

I was keenly focused on making it work, but it was taking a toll on my family and me. I felt that I would not be able to last if I just did these turnarounds, because I was working 60 hours or more a week without break. The stress and strain were significant. I realized that I did not want to just be the turnaround guy and every three or four years I would be in a new turnaround situation. Once this turnaround is completed, I am going to figure out how I continue to add value to the organization. That pivot would become my new focus.

During most of my first two years at CBC, I approved every purchase order for the entire college. Often, I would work late into the night because there was too much to do during the regular workday. So, I would review POs when I went home, sometimes till 10:30 p.m. The next day, I would bring them back to the office and exchange them for the next batch awaiting my review. On weekends, I pored over stacks of budget reports printed on continuous feed, perforated green bar computer paper. I would review every budget line by line. If I could take $25 out of a line, I would.

In the beginning, I micromanaged almost everything. We had good people working at CBC, but many did not have much specific training or background for their positions. So, I modeled effective practices and procedures, like fast-food companies do for their franchisees. McDonald's may do things differently than Burger King, or Wendy's, or Chick-fil-A, but each of these has systems and procedures designed to help their business run smoothly and successfully. At CBC, early on at least, we were going to do things the Ron Ellis way.

After the first few years, as conditions steadily improved, I realized that I needed to delegate more. We all needed to up our game; CBC was going through different iterations because the organization was constantly changing, and people had bought into the vision and process. A culture of change had been accepted. The good news was it was changing by growing and improving, as we soon would see.

I started as president of CBC on November 1, 1994, two months after the official fall enrollment was fixed at 808 students. We had just 10 months to meet the ambitious goal I had set, to increase enrollment to 1,000 students the next fall. In less than a year, our student recruitment process began operating at a very high level. Kent Dacus, director of admissions, and Brian Carroll, dean of the Evening College, and their teams played significant roles in leading this tremendously effective effort.

Fall 1995 enrollment at California Baptist College totaled 1,226, a year-to-year net increase of 418 students. The 51.7% enrollment growth eclipsed both the goal and the examples I had proffered the previous fall. For many, a common reaction to the remarkable increase was amazement.

We commemorated the achievement at the end of September Board of Trustees meeting, where I handed out T-shirts designed with a graph showing the prodigious enrollment increase. We also splurged on a celebratory lunch (including jumbo shrimp!) for employees. Citing the parable recorded in Matthew 20:1-16, I recommended to the board that everyone who was employed at CBC on the board meeting date receive a 10% pay increase, even if they had started working the day before. I wanted the raise to be retroactive to July 1, the start of the fiscal year, or to the employee's start date for anyone hired after July 1. Trustees approved the increase, which hit employee paychecks in the middle of October. For most employees, it was a significant spike because the 10% increase in that paycheck covered July, August, and September.

When we enrolled 1,226 students that fall, I felt there was some breathing room. But I also got back into the saddle knowing that while we had turned a corner, the turnaround was not complete. We did not have to worry about making payroll or paying the utility bills at the end of the month, but we were not there.

In fall 1996, the second year, student enrollment increased to 1,687. I had a feeling that we were really doing something special here. We had developed a strong core of faculty and staff that were operating in a very high and coordinated manner. Even early skeptics were sending me encouraging notes of support. The culture had definitely changed, and positive change became normative. Problem solving and continuous improvement were ingrained. We had different T-shirts made up, did a celebration lunch again, and everybody received an 8% pay raise.

The third year, CBC enrollment went to 2,009. At that point, we had increased the number of students 152% in less than three years. Our budget was close to $25 million, more than double the amount just three years before. By the time we had the third consecutive enrollment increase, the T-shirt thing was getting old. That was the last time we did it. But employees received another 8% pay raise.

In less than three years, CBC employees received pay increases totaling more than 25%, closer to 30% when you consider compounding. That was a tangible demonstration that we were investing in the people who were getting the job done. I think it turned a lot of doubters and people who were just on the fence into believers. It was a great run that firmly reinforced my message: we are all enrollment people, we are all retention people, we are all in the same boat, and we all benefit. A rising tide lifts all boats.

At the outset, some people had questioned the idea of rapid growth at CBC. If we go for quantity, they said, it will harm the quality. I disputed that claim, explaining that we would use quantity to fund quality. And that has been the case for the past three decades. It wasn't easily accepted at the beginning, but as we began to create the funding from the enrollment increases, we invested it back into laboratories and classrooms, faculty and staff. It became very clear that, no, quantity and quality are not in conflict with each other.

A contemporary example of this is the Apple iPhone. I think most people would see Apple as an exemplar of quality, renowned for using high quality materials and making products that are built to last. Apple is also one of the largest companies in the world, quantity-wise. Since introducing the revolutionary iPhone in 2007, Apple has shown that selling more iPhones does not reduce the quality of the device. Quite the contrary, the iPhone has continually improved over time. Each successive generation adds new features and upgrades. Apple enhances iPhone quality by reinvesting some of the surplus revenue generated by the volume (quantity) of sales.

I believed the same principle would apply to CBC, and in relatively short order it proved to be true. Three straight years of robust, three-figure enrollment increases relieved much of the pressure. The growth had not been easy those first three years, but we didn't have to worry about square footage, parking spaces, desks, or classrooms. We had more than enough of just about everything.

After CBC grew from 808 students to 2,009, however, suddenly there was not much of anything that was under capacity; no empty parking spaces, no vacant student housing. There were no empty classrooms or empty offices, and no surplus food service capacity. Everything was impacted, including the institution's ability to continue growing.

Among the people who appreciated the gravity of the situation at CBC early in my presidency, the most important was John Funk, the chair of the board. He was a businessperson with a lot of experience dealing with executives. We would meet often, and he would ask me a number of questions about the plan to transform CBU. I would tell him what we were going to do, and we would drill down into the details. He was extremely supportive and seemed to grasp it all better than most. He had a very strong understanding of the financial situation of CBC. So, as I began to talk about how we were going to turn it around, a lot of it was in terms that translated easily to a business approach.

For instance, when I was interviewing, I talked about analyzing the situation, using a quad chart to evaluate cost and quality at CBC. A quad chart is a visual tool that uses four quadrants to summarize information, each section representing different values: high-low, low-high, high-high, low-low. One of the challenges that I saw was that while CBC essentially was a boutique, it was selling its product at high volume, discount store prices. That doesn't work in higher education unless you have tremendously large third-party pay or a huge endowment; CBC had neither. It had very limited sales, but was trying to compete on price with, say, Walmart. That doesn't work anywhere on the quadrant. We needed to move in specific directions. We had to get our quality and our volume up while holding our price down.

So, for my first four years at CBC, we did not increase tuition. But during that period, enrollment went from 808 to 2,009 in three years' time. When that happened, it was time to make a change. But even then, we only went up 5%, from $300 a unit to $315. Before that, a sizeable group of students had gone through their entire programs at CBC at the same tuition.

Although that tuition increase was modest, it applied to a significantly larger number of students than CBC had when I arrived. That happy combination helped us begin to change the value proposition as we generated more resources. We were able to address deferred maintenance. Buildings were being painted, needed repairs were being made, new furniture and new equipment began arriving. Additional faculty were hired. Quality was going up across the board at CBC. Increasing quantity through higher enrollment was producing the resources needed to increase quality standards. The model worked, and we would continue to work that model at California Baptist University for years to come.

Chapter 13

8080 by 2020 and the Legacy of John Funk

John C. Funk was the Board of Trustees chair and a member of the search committee that recommended me to become the fifth president of California Baptist University. From the beginning, he was instrumental in helping me successfully get off the ground.

John was a devout Southern Baptist layperson from Westlake Village, California. He was active with the Gideons International, an association of Christian business professionals dedicated to telling people about Jesus and best known for placing Bibles and New Testaments in hotels. His business background and wisdom added value as he served multiple terms on the boards of CBU and Golden Gate Baptist Theological Seminary.[9]

We would meet about once a month. Invariably, at the beginning of our meeting, he would ask me, "What can the college do for you and your family?" At first, it seemed like an odd question because I was usually all geared up to talk about issues and strategies. John was very adept with those things, but he also was genuinely

[9] Golden Gate Baptist Theological Seminary was renamed Gateway Seminary of the Southern Baptist Convention in 2016.

concerned about making sure that I wasn't going to be attracted to some other school. It took several months before I eventually wrapped my head around that and realized that I needed to take his opening question seriously. But how should I even answer that question?

As I contemplated how to respond, I spoke with one of my mentors, Dr. Doug Hodo. At the time, he was the president of my alma mater, but I had met him a few years earlier. We got together during an annual meeting of the Southern Baptist Convention. I told him that the chair of my board was asking me what I wanted in my employment contract. I asked Dr. Hodo, 'What should I say?'

He gave me some good advice about things I might want to include in the contract. I appreciated his counsel, and it was helpful as I worked through that employment agreement with the CBC Board of Trustees.

I credit John Funk for his critical understanding and support in those early years.

Dr. Ellis speaks as John Funk looks on in the background

I believe his experience and business acumen helped to make him one of the best that I have ever seen at recognizing executive talent and potential. As time passed, we would develop a strong friendship founded on mutual understanding, trust, and a shared zeal for the Great Commission. Not surprisingly, the Gideons International website prominently displays the text from Matthew 28:19-20. It reminds me how meaningful that Bible passage was to John, just as it has been to me since childhood.

Because I had been active in Southern Baptist life for a long time, I knew where the ditches were, and I made sure we were staying between them. I tried always to be perceptive, proactively considering how California Southern Baptists would react to the plans and changes we were making for CBC. The figure of speech, will this play in Peoria, more aptly became, will this fly in Fresno? I viewed the school's aims and actions through the lens of sensitivity. Through it all, my own sense of mission and the resolute vision I had for CBC never wavered. My purpose was to transform the institution from a struggling Baptist college into a thriving university committed to the Great Commission. I had found historical support for my vision in the institutional mission statement contained in the 1954 Articles of Incorporation. The statement provided two rationales I believed were needed to achieve the turnaround I envisioned. The first would allow adding new disciplines to the liberal arts. This would help reshape the college into a university. The second lent validation to placing the Great Commission at the heart of the institution. What I needed was to be given room to make that vision a reality. John Funk understood that.

"Let him be himself," he urged others on the Board of Trustees. That's what John did, and so did the board. That was a real gift for me. It helped tremendously by not having every idea or action second guessed as we implemented new systems and strategies needed to accomplish the turnaround I had been hired to perform.

John was always thoughtful in the ways we worked together on matters related to the college. He challenged me to visualize not just the next step, but how things might look even years in the future by advancing a potent vision through purposeful action.

In 2004, John was once again serving as the board chair. I would soon mark my 10th anniversary as president. And it was six years since CBC had become California Baptist University, although one could argue the name was still more aspirational than could be documented. Following an executive session of the board, from which even the president is excluded, John and I had a meeting. He told me that he and the board wanted me to re-envision the future of the school.

'Well, give me six months,' I responded. 'I will do a deep dive into the literature, and I will come up with a plan.'

So, for the next six months, while keeping the place going, I studied this challenge every chance I could. Several related questions formed the center of my inquiry. These included: What is a university? What is a reasonable enrollment goal? What is the depth and breadth of program offerings and auxiliary services that would be needed?

I read volumes of material from a variety of sources. I began to think that about 8,000 students, plus or minus, would be a decent target number. I especially looked at several universities in the West Coast Conference, all of them private Christian institutions. I examined their enrollments, academic offerings, and professional programs at both the undergraduate and graduate levels. What I learned from that review strengthened my sense that, give or take a couple of thousand students, 8,000 would be a good size for a school like CBU.

It was becoming clear to me that with 8,000 students and the right mix of programs, it would undeniably be a fine university. Ensuring that the school remained committed to the Great Commission would also differentiate CBU because we were not going to stray from that on my watch.

As I continued my research, I came across an idea that has since become prevalent in education but was then an emerging concept known as STEM. The acronym, STEM, is an umbrella term grouping related academic disciplines: Science, Technology,

Engineering, and Math. I dug deeper to learn if there were any evangelical Christian universities with a lot of STEM programs, but I couldn't find one.

Wow! I thought. That would be a huge differentiator. Not only would STEM go over well in our immediate service area, the Inland Empire of Southern California, but it would also position us regionally. With the right mix of STEM and other new programs, it could even put CBU on the map nationally. Energized by the prospect, my reimagining of the future of CBU started to coalesce around STEM-fueled enrollment growth.

My own background and academic training had given me an appreciation for institutional image and marketing. Among other things, it taught me to admire a simple turn of phrase that succinctly conveys a bold, even audacious vision. In the mid-1970s, Southern Baptists had adopted a program to evangelize the world by the year 2000, which captured my attention. The campaign was called Bold Mission Thrust. Each word in the name carried a vivid, descriptive meaning: "Bold" signified the valiant goal of the ambitious, nearly 25-year program; "Mission" highlighted the Christian mandate for evangelism at its heart; and "Thrust" denoted the concerted push needed to propel the initiative to completion. Bold Mission Thrust was more than a brilliant tagline; it was a call to action that inspired millions of Southern Baptists during the last quarter of the 20th century.

The new vision I had been tasked with developing for CBU would build upon the foundation set by the school's founders in 1950. It would be a blueprint to expand the vision of a university committed to the Great Commission that I had introduced nearly a decade ago. Using a web-based idiom that was gaining popularity, I would be unveiling a vision for CBU 2.0.

To promote this revised vision for the future of the university, I wanted a simple, yet impactful catchphrase that would introduce it and help carry it forward to completion. I am big on numbers as a primary tool for measuring progress, so I started there. CBU had 808 students when I came; a tenfold increase would push that number to 8,080 (read: eighty-eighty). 20/20 is a measurement of vision, and year 20 of the 21st century would be 2020 (read: twenty-twenty). The catchphrase almost wrote itself: "8080 by 2020! The goal was to increase enrollment to 8,080 students by the year 2020. It achieved nearly all the qualities of a SMART goal: it was specific, measurable, relevant, and time-bound. But was it achievable? And if so, how could we do it?

Fall 2004 enrollment totaled 2,359 students. Growing that number to 8,080 over the next 16 years would require an average net increase of 357.6 students per year. That would be more than double the average year-over-year enrollment gain we had recorded at CBU since I became president. That alone was challenging.

But wait, there's more.

Achieving the 8,080 by 2020 enrollment goal would require adding new academic programs, facilities, and services. We would need to increase the number of faculty and other employees. We would need to cultivate donors and find more funding sources to help underwrite the enormous capital investment needed to serve a university the size of the one I was envisioning.

This would be a mammoth undertaking. But carefully crunching the numbers and praying about the project convinced me that, yes, we could do it. The numbers part of it would be demanding, but two scripture passages provided calming assurance. The first was, "Commit your way to the Lord, trust also in Him, and He will do it."[10] The second was, "Trust in the Lord with all your heart and do not lean on your own understanding. In all your ways acknowledge Him, And He will make your paths straight."[11] I knew that achieving the goal would not be easy, but I was confident we could do it.

I believed this renewed vision for the future of CBU, summarized in the catchphrase I had coined, would be a goal we could sink our teeth into. So, I outlined my plan to the trustees at their next meeting. Almost at once, I experienced déjà vu. When I brought up the 8080 by 2020 enrollment target, expressions on the faces of

[10] Psalm 37:5 (NASB)

[11] Proverbs 3:5-6 (NASB)

several trustees were very similar to the response of some when I first came to CBC and said, 'We are going to have a thousand students next fall.' Their eyes just glazed over. They were not opposed to the goal; they just did not understand how it could work. But after further discussion, the Board of Trustees unanimously approved the goal for the university, and we went right to work.

We had only 16 years to make it happen. That sounds like a long time, but there was a lot of work to do. The following fall, enrollment increased by 546 students, exceeding the average net increase I had calculated we would need each year to reach our goal. We were off to a good start. Then, in the next two years we saw smaller increases, each one less than the target average. In all but one of the remaining years, however, CBU recorded strong triple-digit enrollment gains, and even one four-digit year-over-year increase in the student headcount.

Dr. Ellis conducting presidential duties as a speaker at a Hall of Fame event

In 2015, CBU enrollment hit 8,541. We had eclipsed the 8080

by 2020 goal five years ahead of schedule. Sadly, John Funk did not live to see CBU realize the goal he had helped set in motion a decade before. John passed away on November 6, 2004, less than a week after my 10th anniversary as president.

After blowing through the 8080 by 2020 goal, it was time to consider the next step for CBU's continuing growth and development. We reviewed enrollment trends from the past decade and looked at plans already in the works for new programs. Coupled together, those factors suggested that increasing enrollment by 50% over the next 10 years would be a bold but achievable goal. I recommended a "Next Step Goal" to increase enrollment to 12,000 students by 2025. The Board of Trustees approved the recommendation.

In the fall of 2024, enrollment totaled 11,931 students. At the time of this writing, CBU is on track to meet the Next Step Goal on or ahead of schedule.

Over the years, when people ask me how large CBU should grow, they usually want to know, "What is the largest enrollment this university should have?" My answer to that question is that there is no limit on the Great Commission. So, at a university committed to the Great Commission, why would we ever even think about capping enrollment?

I feel certain that John Funk would agree with me on that.

Chapter 14

R. Bates Ivey

R. Bates Ivey became a well-known figure among California Southern Baptist churches and associations during the last half of the 20th century. A native Texan and veteran of World War II in the U.S. Marines, Ivey settled in the Golden State after the war. He served as associate pastor and director of education with Dr. Cecil Pearson, pastor of First Southern Baptist Church of San Diego. During 14 years with that congregation, Ivey also was active in Southern Baptist association and state convention programs and meetings. And after Dr. Pearson became executive secretary of California Baptist Foundation, Ivey was named assistant executive secretary by directors of the agency.[12]

Ivey first served as a California Baptist College trustee from 1983 to 1987. After a four-year hiatus, he returned to the board in 1991 to serve another four-year term. He was one of the trustees who voted unanimously to hire me as president in 1994, and he served on the board for three years afterward.

When I was hired, I made a commitment that during my first 12 months I would be in all the Southern Baptist associations in

[12] California Baptist Foundation was renamed The Baptist Foundation of California in 2017.

the state, from the north to the south. That was a big order, as I would learn. There were 1,279 Southern Baptist churches in 33 associations covering the territory between Oregon and Mexico, and from Nevada and Arizona to the Pacific Ocean.[13] Meeting with pastors and laypeople in each association would take a lot of time, and I had a lot to turn around at CBC. But thanks in large part to Bates Ivey, I kept that commitment. He vigorously encouraged my plan to meet with Baptists in every part of the state. He even offered to accompany me on some of the visits and helped arrange the meetings. He was eager to introduce me to rank and file Baptists across California, and to help me learn about their work in the Golden State.

Bates Ivey was the ideal person to show me around. He was affable, gracious, well-versed about things I wanted to learn and, even in his mid-70's, tireless. Through his work managing the church loan division of the California Baptist Foundation, he had innumerable contacts across the state. That was a big plus as we began my introduction to Southern Baptists in California.

I recall one trip in particular. I had flown into Sacramento, and Ivey met me in his car at the airport. I put my luggage in the trunk, and we started off on a five-day journey. There was no money for the tour, but here is what was great about that: to keep costs down, we would share a room at a budget motel. In the morning, we would get up and have breakfast, usually with directors of missions from the Southern Baptist associations and pastors of churches in the region. A couple of hours later we would have coffee with another group in the next town. These sessions would be repeated with still more new folks over lunch, and sometimes again at an afternoon meeting. Then, we would either have dinner or an evening group meeting with yet another batch of Baptist ministers, laypersons, or both. The next morning, we would get up and start all over again. We did this for five straight days, and it really helped me see what California Southern Baptist work was like.

I had worked at Baptist-affiliated colleges in Texas, Louisiana,

[13] Source: California Southern Baptist Convention 1995 Annual

and Kentucky. All of those have old-line, Southern Baptist state conventions that go way back. For instance, the Kentucky Baptist Convention was formed in 1837. That was eight years before the Southern Baptist Convention, the national denomination, was organized. Many of the older Baptist state conventions are very strong in their financial support for various ministries including colleges and universities. It is not unusual to find churches with large campuses and spacious, well-equipped facilities. Moreover, churches in these states often receive and benefit from the support of mayors, city councils, planning commissions, and others in local government. Many elected officials are church members or regular attenders. Where I came from, there was a lot of cultural support for Baptist churches.

The California Southern Baptist Convention was comparatively young when I arrived. It had been organized in 1940, and many still considered the Golden State to be a pioneer area for Southern Baptist work. One of the first things I noticed about that on my travels across California was that real estate was very, very costly. Also, there were not many Southern Baptists in the nation's most populous state. In 1994, California's population was 31.3 million. The California Southern Baptist Convention reported combined church membership that year totaled fewer than 430,000.

Another thing I learned was that many California counties and municipalities had (and still have) zoning unfavorable to churches. Because churches are tax exempt under state and federal law, they do not directly increase the local tax base. Also, concerns about traffic congestion and noise pollution often present obstacles when churches try to get permits for a new house of worship or to expand existing facilities. I had never heard those issues raised against starting a church in Louisiana, Texas, or Kentucky. People there would almost fall over themselves to help; often, they would either donate land or help build the church. And building codes in the other states where I had lived were not that onerous, so, usually the question was, how can we get this going? In California, I learned, it was often the opposite. Nearly every step in starting a church was oppressive and expensive, beginning with property costs. On top of that, in most places there just weren't that many people naturally disposed to join a church. Consequently, many churches were serving more seekers than believers looking for a church membership experience. The average Southern Baptist church in California had fewer than 340 members in 1994.[14] Most were much smaller. It was clear that these churches would not be able to help CBC financially; they were dealing with their own serious challenges in their local communities.

The time I spent getting acquainted with Southern Baptist churches and associations across the state was eye-opening. It was not negative; rather, it brought me to an unexpected realization. It helped me realize that we would be largely on our own at CBC. I was still intent on working with these churches, but I saw that we would have to make it happen on our own.

One of the wonderful things about the trips I took with Bates Ivey was the time we spent in the car together. For hours, I just picked his brain, and he gave me almost a graduate degree in California Southern Baptist history. He was extremely knowledgeable about Baptist work in California and very forthcoming with what he knew. I was like a sponge, soaking it all up, adding new knowledge to what I had learned before.

On those trips, I learned a lot about the operation of the state Baptist convention, about the churches, and about the interplay with the associations. I also learned how Baptists and their organizations in California viewed the college, both good and bad. Even though I had only been in the state a few months, I arguably had greater in-depth understanding about these things than most people who were Southern Baptist in the state, even those who had been here for a long time. Bates Ivey deserves a lot of credit for helping me gain that understanding during my first year in California. He was tremendously enthusiastic about my vision for a university committed to the Great Commission. When he introduced me, it was almost embarrassing. But it also disarmed people, and then I would talk about the school's vision and what we were going to do. As I had done with

[14] Source: 1994 California Southern Baptist Convention Annual

the CBC board, employees, and other stakeholders, I would describe the rich opportunities I saw in the 1954 Articles of Incorporation. In meetings with Southern Baptists throughout California, I would cite the CBC mission statement as historical support for my vision to build a university committed to the Great Commission.

I cannot overstate how valuable the time spent barnstorming California with Ivey was during that first year as I was working to build enrollment at CBC. I am forever grateful to him for introducing me to people from one end of the state to the other. It was a swift, revealing immersion into the work of Southern Baptists in the Golden State, and it opened my eyes to the challenges and opportunities facing churches large and small.

Following his retirement, the California Baptist Foundation honored our mutual friend and esteemed co-laborer with a gift that helped fund the R. Bates Ivey Plaza on the CBU campus. The plaza, located between buildings in the Lancer Arms complex, is a modest memorial that includes his likeness on a bronze marker.

Milton Higgins, R. Bates Ivey, Lucy Ivey and Dr. Ellis at the dedication of the R. Bates Ivey Plaza at Lancer Arms

That is fitting; modest is an apt description of his personal demeanor and dealings with others. To me, it is a monumental reminder of the impact one can have on others who share a vision in common, even an uncommon one.

Chapter 15

Opportunity Planning

For the past 30 years, enrollment growth has helped California Baptist University in a variety of ways. It has provided funding to increase academic offerings, add and improve facilities, and support continually expanding operations. These and other benefits have validated my conviction that it is possible to leverage quantity to build quality. They also helped shape my pragmatic focus on being nimble and opportunistic.

I have always been a very goal-oriented person, even as a child. For just about everything I ever did, I set a goal to help me achieve it. Goals can provide a sense of purpose and direction. They can improve productivity and measure progress toward achieving a desired outcome. Goals play a big part in my motivation to succeed. But I have also intuitively understood the need for flexibility to avoid getting locked in when something does not work out as planned. My customary process for most initiatives is simple: set a clear goal, accompanied by details, and then be flexible.

I believe it is important to have a goal for anything worth doing. For example, if one is planning a trip, make a list of things to see and do along the way. The list helps with organizing the trip and scheduling planned activities. So, one starts out and the trip unfolds according to plan. But then an unexpected problem causes the third stop to be cancelled. Time to adjust.

When something like that happens to me, I've always been quick to say, 'Well, what else is there here to see or do? Okay, let's do that.' Sometimes the unplanned pivot turns out better than what we thought we wanted to see in the first place. I think part of my success comes from being nimble so I can stay on goal. If a plan doesn't work out because of something beyond my control, I'm not going to waste time and energy beating myself up. Instead, I tend to say, 'Okay, next man up. Let's go!' and keep leaning into the future.

This approach was ingrained when I came to California Baptist College. Based on my research of CBC and its environment, the Board had hired me with the understanding that I would lead the building of a university committed to the Great Commission. But the institution was going to transform from a liberal arts college into a university. It would retain a strong liberal arts component, but the university would rapidly develop large, attractive, in-demand offerings. The Great Commission university would be actualized using my vision of opportunity planning.

While I didn't come up with the idea of opportunity planning, I applied my experiences and made it my own. My version draws from the earthly ministry of Christ as recorded in the red letters. Red-letter Bibles are editions of the Bible with the words of Jesus Christ printed in red ink, making them easier for readers to identify. As I read the red letters, it strikes me that Jesus' modus operandi is not to tell his followers every move. He doesn't tell the apostles, "At 11 o'clock, at the corner of Magnolia and Adams, I'll be healing lepers and the blind." No, that's not what he says.

There is an as-you-go aspect to Christ's ministry, which I find very significant. Examples of this approach are recorded in all three synoptic Gospels. One is the occasion when Jesus is walking down the road and a woman with a chronic ailment comes up to him and touches his garment, hoping to be healed.[15] Jesus stops and has a brief conversation with the woman. Then he tells her, "Your faith has

[15] Matthew 9:20-22

made you whole." In a random encounter as he was walking along the road, Jesus ministered to a stranger.

Another example of Christ's as-you-go ministry method takes place in Capernaum. Jesus is teaching a large crowd when four men arrive, carrying a paralyzed man on a mat.[16] The men cannot get inside the house because of the crowd, so they carry the man up the outside stairs to the flat roof of the one-story house. They break through the roof tiles to make a large enough opening to lower the man down. When Jesus sees the men's faith, he says to the paralyzed man, "Son, your sins are forgiven." Interrupting a teaching session, Jesus performs a healing.

Only one miracle of Jesus is recorded in all four Gospels. The accounts describe Christ trying to get away from the crowd to go on a retreat.[17] But the throngs follow him. As thousands gather, Jesus sees a teachable moment. Just then, the Apostles come to him and ask, where are we to buy meat that these may eat? This is not a planned event. The disciples are not prepared for the multitude that has gathered to see Jesus. There is not enough food. But in this teachable moment, Jesus blesses a boy's five barley loaves and two fish and administers the feeding of 5,000 people. Or, as I like to say, fish tacos for everybody!

Those are examples of the way it's presented in the scriptures, and the way I look at it, it is "as you go." And here is what I glean from that: Christ's earthly ministry was a combination of things like teaching, healing, meeting, and ministering to the needs of people. But it doesn't seem to have been a rigid plan. It was more like as you go, opportunities present themselves. A key aspect of my version of opportunity planning is looking for opportunities to minister to unmet needs. One sees what one is looking for. Jesus was constantly looking for opportunities to minister and therefore he readily recognized them when others did not. During his earthly ministry, he modeled looking for opportunities to serve and then

---

[16] Luke 5:17-39

[17] Matthew: 14:13-21; Mark: 6:30-44; Luke: 9:12-17; John: 6:1-13.

meeting the needs that were presented. I focused on that in my scripture reading and thought hard about that.

In graduate school, I read about Japan's economic turnaround in the second half of the 20th century. If you would have said, 'describe Japanese products' in 1960, people likely would have said cheap, low quality, and low tech. If you would have said 'describe Japanese products' in 1979, responses likely would have been high quality, high tech, and moderate price. What makes the change even more remarkable is that this wasn't a company; it was a country. This was Japan, Inc., and I was fascinated with that.

When I read how Japan achieved its economic turnaround, I found that it was the result of a very formulaic, strictly disciplined approach. It was sharply focused on using principles, techniques, and tools for process improvement that aimed at constantly making things more efficient. So, as I developed my own style, it morphed from my exposure to the red letters and Japan, Inc.

As part of my 150 hours of study preparing for the on-campus interview for the open position of president, I came across the institutional mission statement articulated in the 1954 Articles of Incorporation:

> "The primary purpose of this corporation is to conduct regular four-year college courses in education, music, sciences and the liberal arts, and to grant certificates, diplomas and any and all degrees evidencing completion of any course of training, together with any and all honorary degrees and to provide training for Baptist youth and others desiring to be affiliated with Baptist theology and theological instruction and such other instruction as may be needful and advantageous in preparing and qualifying ministers and others for Christian work."

I found it intriguing and a wonderful fit for my vision to build a university committed to the Great Commission. In the first section,

I saw the rationale for expanding academics well beyond the liberal arts. As I examined the statement in detail, I noted that liberal arts were included in the list but after education, music, and the sciences. This did not seem accidental since liberal arts were not listed in alphabetical order or in the first position. Furthermore, the statement continued to list future possibilities via "certificates, diplomas, and any and all degrees evidencing completion of any course of training." I understood the inclusion of the word "training" to expand even further into practical areas such as technology, health sciences, architecture, aviation, graphic design, and beyond.

Additionally, the last part of the mission statement specifically emphasized "training for Baptist youth and others desiring to be affiliated with Baptist theology and theological instruction and such other instruction as may be needful and advantageous in preparing and qualifying ministers and others for Christian work." In this section, I saw the rationale for the Great Commission being at the heart of the institution, because I believe Baptists are at their best when they focus on the Great Commission. I shared this conviction in several interview sessions, including with the search committee and the full Board of trustees, as well as in a meeting with the faculty, and in sessions with other stakeholders around the state.

From the outset, I was focused on the fact that CBC is a faith-based institution–a college, not a business. With that perspective, we would need to pay more attention to the ministry aspect of the institution and do more opportunity planning. When I was preparing to interview for the position at CBC in 1994, I knew I would need to put a turnaround plan together. But to do that I needed to know the context. I needed to understand the geographic area called the Inland Empire. I needed to know the history of California. What is the higher education situation? I found that it was unique from any others I had experienced. As a practitioner of opportunity planning, I developed a detailed plan, but it did not say, here are the five academic programs we're going to start. Instead, I came with the intention of looking at the market to figure out where there were gaps.

If you and I were going into business together, the normal way we would begin is by developing a business plan. We would decide what products or services the business was going to offer. We would list our respective strengths, passions, and interests and figure out what our roles will be. We would try to agree on what we are going to do and how we're going to do it, and then that's what we are going to do.

Opportunity planning is essentially 180 degrees different from that. I think here is where the power lies. First, we're going to focus on a very small number of things that we're not going to do. This is very important. For CBU, two examples are alcohol and hospitality.

California Baptist University is a conservative Baptist institution in a very secular state. California vineyards and wineries account for more than 80% of the wine produced in the United States. Some of the best viticulture (study of grape cultivation) programs in the United States, if not the world, are in California. Winemaking titans Robert Mondavi and E.&J. Gallo have given significant financial support to the viticulture and enology (study of wine and winemaking) program at the University of California, Davis. Similar undergraduate programs are offered at California State University, Fresno, and California Polytechnic State University, San Luis Obispo. Several community colleges in the Golden State award associate degrees in viticulture and enology. The growth of California's wine industry has increased the demand for such programs. But because of Baptists' historic emphasis on abstinence, CBU is not going to offer that. We are not being judgmental about it; we are just saying that we are not going to pursue that program.

The second example of what CBU is not going to do involves hospitality, a segment of tourism. California's tourism industry is one of the nation's largest with total revenues exceeding $150 billion in 2023.[18] Hospitality helped generate state and local tax revenues totaling more than $12.5 billion the same year and supported

---

[18] Dean Runyon Associates, Inc. Economic Impact of Travel in California 2014-2023. Accessed August 28, 2024.
https://industry.visitcalifornia.com/research/economic-impact.

approximately 1.2 million jobs in the state. Many such jobs are at popular tourist destinations not far from the California Baptist University campus in Southern California. Again, because of CBU's conservative Christian values, we're saying two things. First, we are not going to offer programs in viticulture, wine production, brewing, or anything of that kind. Second, we will not offer a program in hospitality, since the food and beverage segment involves beer, wine, and spirits. We are not saying that hospitality is bad; we're simply saying that because of who we are, and given our traditional, conservative, historical Baptist ties and values, we're just not going to do that.

Now, here's the power of opportunity planning. Once you know the handful of things that you're not going to do, everything else is fair game. It is not about what you or I particularly are interested in; it's what pencils financially, and what the market is telling us that it wants and needs.

When I came to CBC, it would have done no good to ask me, what are the top five programs you're going to start? You would have missed the point. I didn't think that way. Before we start any new programs, we're going to look at the market. If there's a real need for a program, and it fits us, and we can make it work, then we're going to go for it. We're not going to put artificial limits on it. We're going to say, here's the academic standard you need to hit, and here's what we're going to offer. If you hit that standard, then it's incumbent upon us to provide it for whoever wants to come for that program within our context.

Early on, we're going to spend most of our energy rapidly increasing enrollment, because that's the fuel that drives the institution. Money is lacking. We don't have a donor base that we can consistently depend on. So, we're going to get creative. We're going to roll our sleeves up, get to work, and we're going to make this happen.

One of my heroes years ago was a fellow named Paul Neal "Red" Adair. The namesake company that he started in Houston was famous for putting out fires and capping oil well blowouts around the globe. Adair is credited with fighting thousands of fires, such as the 1988 Piper Alpha North Sea disaster that had claimed 167 lives. Three years later, Red Adair Company helped extinguish hundreds of oil wells set ablaze in Kuwait by retreating Iraqi forces during the Gulf War.[19]

Red Adair would go virtually anywhere and battle any oil well fire. Typically, oil rig blowouts burn violently out of control and are extremely difficult to extinguish. Unchecked, they burn and burn, and what they are burning is money. Oil companies would call Adair about putting out a fire at a production site. He would tell them what he would do and what it would cost. More than once, oil company executives would choose to let a blowout continue to burn for weeks, but to no avail. Then, when they agreed to hire Adair's company, he would tackle the job and in a very short order the fire was out.

I think it bothered some of Adair's clients that his company got the job done so quickly. They felt like they had overpaid or been cheated. But no, what they paid was the value of the service Adair had provided. He knew he was the expert, and he had the record to back it up. He had kind of a secret sauce. He knew how to do what most people could not do. That rare talent would have allowed Adair to say, in effect, when you get ready to have your oil rig fire put out, just give me a call.

I had a lot of theory about how to do organizational change when I came to CBC. I had already put myself into some situations where I had helped to change organizations. I also had been in some situations where I realized, 'Boy, this is not the way to do it, but they are not ready for change. The conditions for success are not present.'

I came to CBC to turn it around. My goal was to be the president of a struggling Baptist college before I was 40, and I had made it at 38. I also had realized that achieving my goal likely would require me to go to a struggling college because those probably were the only ones that would be interested in somebody like me. But that is what I wanted to do. I was not interested in being a serial president. I just

[19] Knight, Gib. "Hellfighters: The Red Adair Story." Accessed August 26, 2024. https://www.oklahomaminerals.com/hellfighters-red-adair-story

wanted to turn around one college, and if CBC happened to be the opportunity, that would be great.

So, like Red Adair in a way, I felt that if you want me to put out the fire, then call me. If not, if you just want to talk about it and try to do it as a committee, then y'all go right ahead and see how that works. I don't mean that in an egotistical way; it was just that I felt like I was an expert. I know how to do this, but for me to be able to do it, I've got to do it my way.

Looking back on these nearly 30 years, I am grateful to the Board of Trustees for allowing that to happen. I think the ability to live my purpose—and frankly, to live my dream—and for that dream to be an unfolding dream, all goes back to one thing. It is the inspiration that I brought to CBU: the vision to build a university committed to the Great Commission.

Chapter 16

The Impact of Athletics

The role of intercollegiate athletics in higher education varies from one institution to the next. For many colleges and universities, however, athletics is both important and impactful for several reasons. At California Baptist University, the upward trajectory of athletics has been an intentional and purposeful pursuit since my arrival in 1994.

Prior to becoming president of CBC, I had had experiences at several institutions where I saw how athletics can be used to enhance campus culture for residential students and others. Whether students take part in college sports as student athletes or attend as fans, athletics provides them with activities that build unity across the campus. It also reaches out to the community. It provides a reason for people to visit the campus almost year-round, helping to build the institution's brand, especially in a small area.

Coming to CBC, I had those experiences in the back of my mind. I knew what athletics could contribute to the turnaround effort we were undertaking. And as we looked at the situation here, it was clear to me that we could use athletics to help build enrollment. I knew from experience that for a college with low enrollment to get a boost and enhance campus culture, starting athletic programs is a good way to do it. So, at my first board meeting, which was held my fourth and fifth days serving as president, I brought two recommendations. My first recommendation was to remove 'interim' from Dr. Bonnie Metcalf's Vice President of Academic Affairs title. The second was to start a track and field team. Both recommendations were approved.

At that point we were using the track and field teams mainly to boost enrollment but also to build campus culture. These teams were practicing at local high school and community college facilities because we did not have a track on our campus.

The first priority is to make sure that the program is competitive. Often in National Association of Intercollegiate Athletics (NAIA) or even National Collegiate Athletics Association (NCAA) Division II institutions, the coach is not a full-time job. Coaches may be full-time employees, but when I arrived at CBC, I found some head coaches were not employed full-time. One of the first steps in building a competitive athletics program is to make sure that head coaches in as many sports as possible are full-time employees. Once they are full-time employees, making each one a 100% full-time head coach helps ensure that they are putting their entire focus on coaching. In my experience, this is crucial from a competitive standpoint.

The next step would be to have a full-time assistant coach. So, first make sure the head coach has an assistant. This may start out as a part-time position, but it should become full-time as soon as possible. At that point, the program will have both a full-time head coach and a full-time assistant coach. That means two full-time positions focused on preparing, recruiting, and coaching. That's a big step. Next, other things like program budgets and facilities need to be enhanced. And as we continued to increase the enrollment and expand the overall operating budget, the additional funds became available.

I tend to want to play up as opposed to play down. In boxing this is called punching above your weight. The phrase is used figuratively to describe someone who competes outside of their comfort zone or usual class. It also describes an entity that succeeds in an activity that requires more resources than it seems to have.

I came to CBC in November of 1994, so my first full academic year was 1995-96. CBC attained university status in 1998 and the following year, California Baptist University emerged as a national power in the National Association of Intercollegiate Athletics (NAIA).

In 1999, CBU won its first two NAIA national championships, in men's track and field and men's volleyball. Overall, the Lancers won 22 team championships in the NAIA era and were runner-up nearly as many times. Nine additional national titles were in the National Christian College Athletic Association during the Lancers' two-year transition from the NAIA to the NCAA Division II in the 2011-12 and 2012-13 seasons.[20] The CBU men's track and field program also captured 18 individual national titles between 1996 and 1999. To date, scholar athletes have won 170 individual national championship titles in women's golf, men's and women's swimming and diving, men's and women's distance running, and wrestling. Heavyweight Joe Fagiano won the CBU wrestling program's first NCAA title at the Division II Championships in 2016.

In 1998, CBU built one of the largest and finest collegiate aquatics centers in the Inland Empire.

[20] California Baptist University. "National Championship Teams." Accessed September 2, 2024. https://cbulancers.com/sports/2020/8/5/national-championship-teams.aspx.

California Baptist University's new Lancer Aquatic Center opened in 1998

We started an aquatics program and became very competitive right away. Between 2005 and 2011, the start of the transition to NCAA D-II, CBU was a dominant power in NAIA men's and women's swimming and diving, winning nine national championships.

During the 1990's, many NAIA member institutions had around 800 to 1,000 students. A few outliers had larger enrollments, but CBC was typical with 808 students when I arrived in 1994. Most NCAA Division II schools have fewer than 8,000 students and when we decided to move to D-II, CBU was still short of that number. But we were closer to it than the typical NAIA number, and we were growing rapidly. So, it made a lot of sense to me to play up, to go ahead and make the transition.

Teams applying for NCAA membership must take a multi-year postseason ineligibility period. They may apply for a waiver to shorten or waive this period, but it's rare for the NCAA to grant one. During CBU's transition to D-II, the Lancers competed postseason in the National Christian College Athletic Association. It was CBU's second membership in the NCCAA, following a 15-year stint that ended in 1987. Rejoining NCCAA while moving to D-II afforded Lancer teams the opportunity of postseason play, which is important for recruiting and for the student athletes' overall experience. In two years, seven CBU teams racked up nine NCCAA national championships.

And we also were benchmarking along the way. As CBU prepared to move from NAIA into NCAA Division II, and later into Division I, all those years we kept track of our record against D-I programs. Even when it was competing as a member of the NAIA, CBU was fielding strong teams in several sports. We often played against NCAA schools, and we would take on any Division I program that would play us in any sport. We also played teams from D-II and D-III, including one contest where CBU's NAIA men's basketball program came out on the winning end of an inglorious NCAA scoring record.

On December 10, 2004, the Lancers traveled to Redlands, California for a game against the D-III University of Redlands Bulldogs. The head coach of the host team, Gary Smith, was known for employing pressure defense, fast breaks, and a run-and-gun pace of play. The Bulldogs averaged 132.4 points per game in 2004-05, the most of any team in Smith's 36-year coaching tenure at Redlands. The Bulldogs would exceed that average against the Lancers, but it would not be enough to deny CBU an upset victory on Redlands' home court.

It was an early season game. CBU had compiled a 7-1 record at that point; Redlands' record was 6-2. I was among the visiting Lancer fans intrigued by Redlands' high-scoring reputation. Who doesn't want to see all that scoring? I'd guess most of the 356 fans in attendance were hoping to see their team put up big numbers that night, and they were not disappointed. I was worn out just watching. Despite the Bulldogs' pressure defense approach, there was almost no defense. The Lancers and Bulldogs took advantage of the 3-point shot that had been approved for college hoops in 1986. On both ends of the court, it was score, score, score!

While the Redlands team was living up to its high-scoring reputation, the Lancers, under head coach Tim Collins, were more than keeping pace. Collins had prepared his team in practices that year and the Lancers were ready. The game started fast paced and never slowed down. CBU drew first blood with a field goal just four seconds into the contest, taking an early 2-0 lead. Redlands answered 10 seconds later, dropping in the Bulldogs' first 3-pointer of the night. From then on, it was a shootout. At halftime, the score looked like the final tally at many collegiate basketball games. CBU was leading, 93-66.

The Bulldogs pushed back hard in the final period, coming within one point of equaling the Lancers' second-half production. But the Redlands comeback bid was too little, too late. When the 40-minute scoring frenzy ended and the final buzzer sounded, CBU had won an incredible 181-156 decision over Redlands. With their loss, the Bulldogs went into the NCAA D-III record books for scoring the most points in a losing effort.[21]

It was one of five victories that season in which the Lancers scored more than 100 points. The 2004-05 CBU men's basketball team posted a season record of 24-10 and played into the Sweet 16 round of the NAIA National Tournament. CBU, still in the NAIA, would go on to an undefeated 6-0 historical record against the D-III Bulldogs. But the Lancers' 2004 "W" at the University of Redlands is still one of the most memorable experiences in CBU athletics.

The CBU men's volleyball team produced another record-setting memory in the Lancers' NAIA era by defeating a top-ranked Division I team for only the second time in history. The first time that had happened was on December 23, 1982, when the Silverswords basketball team at tiny Chaminade University in Honolulu defeated the unbeaten and No. 1 ranked University of Virginia Cavaliers. The feat seemed even more incredible since the Cavaliers' lineup included 7'4" Ralph Samson. A future NBA Hall of Fame standout, Samson was already a two-time national player of the year; he would win that honor three times, a feat equaled by only one other player, Bill Walton of UCLA.

Chaminade's unthinkable 77-72 upset took place as Virginia was returning from a trip to Japan, and after the Cavaliers had trounced

[21] NCAA.com.http://fs.ncaa.org/Docs/stats/m_basketball_RB/2011/D3.pdf

the Silverswords in two earlier meetings.[22] It was an amazing thing for Chaminade, an NAIA school at the time, to defeat Virginia, the number one ranked NCAA Division I team. First off, how many times would an NAIA team even play a top-ranked D-I opponent? I can tell you; it doesn't happen often. So, that record, an NAIA school knocking off an NCAA Division I number one ranked team, stood for nearly 25 years.

Then, almost a quarter century later, California Baptist University, an NAIA school at the time, hosted the number one ranked men's volleyball team from D-I Brigham Young University. CBU had a tremendous men's volleyball team in that era and had already won five NAIA national championships. Number six would follow later that year. In all, the Lancers men's volleyball program would win eight NAIA national championships in 13 years. Like I said, they were good!

On February 13, 2007, I was one of nearly a thousand fans packed into CBU's Van Dyne Gym for a regular-season game against BYU. It seemed like at least 70% of the seats held fans rooting for the visitors. When CBU won the first set over the top ranked Cougars from BYU, it felt like my breathing was becoming more difficult. I remember thinking this is really happening, and hoping nothing would happen to jinx it. Nothing did, and CBU knocked off BYU, 3-0 (30-25, 30-23, 31-29).[23]

[22] Lopresti, Mike. "The unthinkable upset, 40 years later: Chaminade shocks No. 1 Virginia in 1982." Accessed September 5, 2024. https://www.ncaa.com/news/basketball-men/article/2022-12-23/unthinkable-upset-40-years-later-chaminade-shocks-no-1-virginia-1982.

[23] CBULancers.com. "NAIA No. 1 Men's Volleyball Defeats NCAA No. 1 BYU." Accessed September 5, 2024. https://cbulancers.com/story.aspx?filename=Moment_No_2&file_date=6/27/2013&path=general

California Baptist University's men's volleyball team huddles in celebration after their victory against Brigham Young University, the NCAA No. 1 ranked team

Such a monumental inter-league collegiate sports upset had happened only one time before, when Chaminade defeated Virginia on the basketball court. This time, CBU was the David that slew the D-I men's volleyball giant, BYU. Looking back on that event, I remember, wow! That was a very special achievement.

From the start of my presidency, we have been focused on realizing the vision of CBU as a university committed to the Great Commission. As soon as it became possible, we began adding programs that have high barriers to entry, such as nursing, engineering, and aviation science, to name a few. Just as we wanted to exhibit excellence in academic programming, we also pursued excellence in athletics. We wanted CBU to be a regional, if not a national or even international brand. The pursuit of excellence in all we do is motivated by the Christian values that CBU has promoted since its founding and inspired by Jesus's instruction to serve "the least of these", as if potentially serving Christ himself.[24] So, with those aspirations, as soon as we were able to make it work, we went to the next level in intercollegiate athletics. When we arrived at the point where the time was right to apply for D-II, we did it at the first opportunity.

While advancing from one level of collegiate athletic competition to the next, the CBU athletics program has consistently benchmarked its performance against higher echelons. Through the years as CBU prepared to move from NAIA into NCAA Division II, and later into Division I, we kept track of our record against D-I programs. We had a winning record overall before applying to D-I.

When I came to CBU, the title of one of my early chapel messages was, We Are Ready, and it wasn't an idle boast. When Jane and I moved to California, we did our homework and prepared for the move. We felt strongly that the conditions for success were present.

From the start, that same kind of getting-all-your-ducks-in-a row preparation and implementation has played out in virtually every area at CBU. It occurred in academics the year after I arrived when we launched the Master of Education degree program; right out of the box we enrolled 63 students. Going forward, when we start new programs such as nursing or engineering, we always try to understand what it will take to be a strong program in both quality and enrollment. When we decide those things and make sure the market is there, then we hire a champion to drive the program. Once you do all those things, unless you miss something, invariably it's going to succeed and it's going to succeed big. So, we do the same thing with athletics. We're benchmarking and putting everything in order not because somebody is requiring that we do these things, but because it makes us competitive. To this day, the intent is to be competitive and to perform at a high level in all areas.

As CBU moved into Division II, its athletics teams were competitive straight out of the chute. We were already looking ahead to Division I, the pinnacle of college sports. When the transition period ended, D-II member institutions had to wait five years before

[24] Matthew 25:40-45

applying for D-I membership. As soon as that waiting period ended, CBU submitted its application.

CBU was remarkably competitive during its Division II era (2013-14 to 2017-18), qualifying 66 of 94 eligible teams for NCAA postseason play. Lancers also won seven individual NCAA national championships, with four in swimming and three in wrestling. Because of these successes, the Lancers began climbing the rankings for the D-II Learfield Directors' Cup. The annual award given by the National Association of Collegiate Directors of Athletics recognizes colleges and universities with the most success in collegiate athletics. Awards are given to the top schools in each of the three NCAA divisions, the National Junior College Athletic Association, and the NAIA.[25] It is based on a point system related to the highest national finishes of seven men's and seven women's sports.

CBU debuted at No. 26 in the Division II Learfield Directors' Cup rankings in 2013-14, the first year as a full member of D-II. In succeeding years, CBU steadily advanced to 16th, fourth and second place in the Learfield Directors' Cup rankings. In 2017-18, its final year in Division II, CBU won the Learfield Directors' Cup for the best overall athletics program among 268 D-II schools in the nation. And then as we exit, we're the number one program in Division II. My assessment would be that the top 10 schools in many sports in Division II are better than the bottom half of the teams in Division I. CBU had played several D-I legacy teams that might have had 3,000 students and not a very big budget, yet they had been Division I for a good while. So, a school like CBU coming in with enrollment and revenue two times as large, and with great facilities and the budget to support it all, would be much more competitive. CBU had played several of these schools, so we knew we were competitive.

In 2023-24, just our second year eligible for D-I postseason play, the Lancers earned a Learfield Directors' Cup ranking of 86th among 364 D-I institutions. Among non-football institutions, CBU ranked 5th, and the Lancers finished 2nd among Western Athletic Conference member institutions. It was a year of strong performances, with

[25] CBU placed fifth in the NAIA Learfield Directors Cup standings in 2008-09.

Lancer teams winning four conference championships and nine teams reaching the NCAA postseason.[26]

NCAA Division I is the highest level of amateur athletics in the United States and includes world-class programs. Many of these programs also reap huge financial gains. In 2022, each of the top 49 D-I programs generated more than $100 million in revenue just from their media rights, ticket sales, merchandise, and donations.[27] The top five programs in that group raked in more than double that amount annually. The number one program, The Ohio State University, took in more than a quarter of a billion dollars in 2022.

The vast majority of Olympians on Team USA have played in NCAA programs. For example, 11 of 12 players on the 2024 U.S.A. Olympic basketball team previously played in the NCAA. LeBron James, the lone exception, was drafted into the NBA directly out of high school. The U.S. Olympic and Paralympic Committee reported on the impact of collegiate sports leading up to the 2024 Paris Olympics:

The American collegiate athletics system plays a vital role in Team USA's success on the Olympic stage. This summer in Paris, 75% of U.S. Olympians will have competed collegiately as part of their journey to Team USA. In total, 169 schools from 45 different conferences will have one or more U.S. Olympians competing in Paris. Twenty-one teams have at least 80% collegiate participation on their U.S. Olympic rosters, including 15 teams that are comprised 100% of collegiate athletes. College athlete representation on the 2024 U.S. Olympic Team spans all three NCAA Divisions (I, II and III), as well as junior colleges, NAIA schools and collegiate club programs.[28]

---

[26] Collom, Ryley. "CBU Finishes 86th overall, 2nd Among WAC Schools in Final LEARFIELD Standings." Accessed September 2, 2024. https://cbulancers.com/sports/2020/8/5/national-championship-teams.aspx.

[27] USA Today. "NCAA Finances: Revenue and Expenses by School." Accessed September 3, 2024. https://sportsdata.usatoday.com/ncaa/finances.

[28] U.S. Olympic and Paralympic Committee. "2024 Qualified U.S. Athletes." Accessed September 3, 2024. https://www.usopc.org/team-usa-2024-collegiate-olympic-footprint.

Many Olympic athletes from other countries also have played at an NCAA program in the United States. One such athlete who competed in Paris was Bul Kuol, who played basketball at California Baptist University from 2016 to 2020. CBU was a D-II program when Kuol started. Two years later, the transition to Division I began. Kuol was recruited to CBU from Australia. In Paris, he was a standout player for the Olympic team from his native South Sudan, which lost to the eventual gold medal-winning USA basketball men's Olympic team.

Division I is very competitive, both nationally and globally. So, with CBU growing as a university in comprehensive academic programming, enrollment, and budget, to me it was the natural thing to advance to D-I. The goal was for the CBU athletic program to reflect the growth and vigor of the university itself.

A college or university's athletic program, rightly or wrongly, has been called the institution's front porch. That often means that more news articles are going to be written about the institution's athletic program than everything else combined. A university might have a stellar physics department or some other exceptional academic program. Such programs might even receive occasional publicity. But in many places, nearly every game in the athletic program is going to be reported. Those reports are probably going to appear in print or online or both. Scores from many Division I athletic programs appear on the ESPN BottomLine, the lower third sports information ticker on all the company's broadcast and streaming channels. There is simply no academic equivalent that I'm aware of for that. So, just from a publicity and marketing standpoint, having a strong NCAA athletic program can place a school's name and brand out there in a very positive way. Of course, it also has the potential to go the other direction. But I think it's undeniable that athletics is a front porch for the institution. College sports are great for community relations and wonderful for building campus culture for residential students.

Once institutions reach a certain size, they no longer need athletics to help build enrollment. As a school grows larger, the percentage of enrollment represented by student athletes declines rapidly. When I arrived at CBC, there were 808 students including around 150 athletes. That was a significant percentage. Today, by comparison, CBU has close to 12,000 students and 400 student athletes. Even comparing that number of athletes with the 3,400 students who live on campus, the percentage is much lower than it was in 1994. It's not a huge amount. But if you have 150 student athletes in a total enrollment of 808, and half of the 300 students who live on campus are athletes, that's a bit heavy. So, we used athletics to help jumpstart enrollment for a few years. As new academic offerings came online and enrollment grew rapidly, athletics was primarily a campus culture value-add. We have been able to do that at CBU so that we are no longer dependent on athletics for enrollment.

To show how ready CBU was for NCAA Division I, during one of the years in transition from D-II the Lancer women's basketball team accomplished something that almost never happens. They went undefeated in the 2020-21 regular season, and then they won their first Western Athletic Conference tournament championship, also without a loss. Just by winning the WAC tournament they would have been eligible for the automatic qualifier bid to the NCAA national tournament, except that CBU was still in transition to D-I. So, because of the transition ban on postseason play, they were denied the opportunity to compete in the NCAA women's tournament. The denial was reported nationally by ESPN and other media outlets that questioned the fairness of the NCAA postseason ban on teams in transition.

That unfortunate situation was a big disappointment for the CBU women's basketball team and fans. The Lancers played in an alternate postseason tournament and won a couple of games before their only loss in an otherwise flawless season. It had been an amazing run and proved beyond a doubt that CBU was ready for Division I.

Since then, CBU has become eligible for NCAA postseason play as a full member of Division I. Last year the women's basketball team won the WAC automatic qualifier again.

CBU women's basketball team celebrates winning the WAC Championship and earning the automatic qualifier to compete in the NCAA's March Madness Tournament
Photo Credit: Lucas Peltier/Western Athletic Conference

They were not the only Lancers team in postseason tournament action. The CBU men's soccer team did something unprecedented by a men's soccer team in the WAC, and this is a very old conference. In the program's first two years of eligibility, the Lancers' men's soccer team won the automatic qualifier for the conference tournament champions in back-to-back seasons. In the second year, the CBU team won a first-round game in the NCAA National Tournament. That was enormously significant for the university.

The 2023 CBU men's soccer team celebrates the conference's first ever back-to-back win and the automatic qualifier to the NCAA tournament
Photo Credit: Lucas Peltier/Western Athletic Conference

CBU also has had a lot of success with the track and cross-country teams. Both men's and women's cross-country teams competed in the postseason during the first year of eligibility. The women's cross-country team made the national race, which features the top 31 teams in the country. That was quite a feather in the Lancers' cap. In 2023-24, the second year of eligibility, both the men's and women's teams competed in those national championship races. At one point late in the year, the CBU men were ranked fourth in the nation. And both CBU teams finished in the top 20 in the races at the end of the year out of 350 teams that compete in cross-country at the Division I level.

Individual Lancers also are finding success at the highest levels of NCAA competition. Greta Karinauskaite, one of CBU's female distance runners, was named First Team All-American at Nationals after a 2nd place finish in the Steeplechase Finals the first year of eligibility.

CBU track athlete Greta Karinauskaite competes at the NCAA Championship

CBU also had two wrestlers who competed in the NCAA Nationals. Hunter Leake became the first Lancer to qualify for D-I Nationals with an automatic bid in the 2023-24 season. Elijah Griffin earned an at-large bid to Nationals, where he earned the Lancers first-ever match wins at Nationals the same year.

To attain and sustain excellence, investment is required, as is internal accountability. Key to success are coaches who can be effective at these levels and who can recruit and field competitive teams. Fortunately for CBU, Southern California is arguably one of the richest areas for athletic talent in the nation. California's population totals nearly 40 million. More than 22 million people inhabit Southern California with nearly 13 million residents in the LA Basin alone, so there's plenty of top-quality athletics. And of course, you're not restricted to just that geographical region for recruiting athletes.

In addition to offering abundant athletic talent, the region's huge population also generates quite a large demand for quality programming. So, if a university like CBU is going to do something in athletics and wants people to come watch, there's almost no limitation on what can be done here. Providing a price-sensitive, family-friendly game day experience can positively contribute to the institution and community. CBU is positioning itself in the Inland Empire as a home team exemplar.

The weather is another positive feature for athletics in Southern California. No matter what sport you are talking about, weather conditions here are amenable to year-round sporting events. Even traditional indoor sports can be staged outdoors, as CBU grapplers showed in history-making fashion on November 15, 2014. The Lancers' inaugural outdoor wrestling match with Stanford University was billed as "Take It Outside." The *al fresco* dual attracted a standing-room-only crowd of 2,620 fans. It was held on the CBU Front Lawn, which also hosts the Fortuna Bowl intramural flag football championships each year. Held during Parent and Family Weekend in November, the Fortuna Bowl is one of the largest events at California Baptist University.

CBU's front lawn transforms for Fortuna Bowl

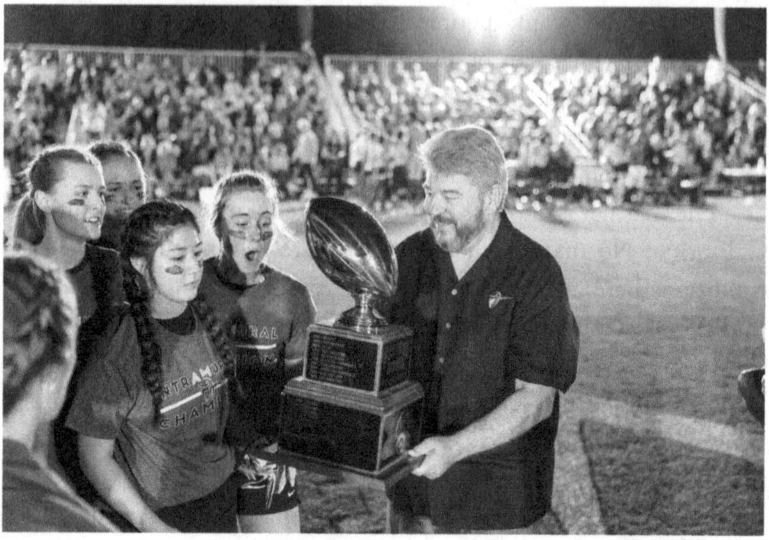

Dr. Ellis awards the Fortuna Bowl Champions their trophy

For the student athletes and their parents, and for other students and fans, events like this create lasting memories and help to build the brand. Fond memories of alma mater are important for these stakeholders. And their fond memories are important for alma mater. That's because satisfied students graduate and become alumni, and satisfied alumni often become donors. They also influence new generations of students to attend their alma mater and encourage others to financially support the institution. In this way, athletics can play an important role in ensuring the university's sustainability.

Founded in 1950, CBU is now in its eighth decade. No two decades are ever the same. The 50s were different than the 60s. The 60s were different than the 70s, and so on. My third decade as president has differed greatly from the two that preceded it. It is good to remember the past, honor the guiding principles and those who faithfully served in bygone eras, and embrace whatever lessons can be learned from experience so that we don't need to repeat them. For example, a key lesson that was reinforced from the COVID-19 pandemic is, we're never going back to the past. The pandemic was a black swan event that altered the global human experience, influencing thought and behavior going forward. So, it is crucial to be nimble because things are always changing.

Right now, there is tremendous change in collegiate ranks with NIL (Name, Image, and Likeness), paid players, and the transfer portal. Athletics scholarship limits have been drastically increased so that every position is now eligible for a full ride. That is in sharp contrast with the past when there were numerous partial scholarships for athletes. For example, NCAA wrestling programs were authorized a maximum of 9.9 equivalent full-ride scholarships. Baseball was authorized 11.7 equivalent full rides. Who comes up with these odd numbers? Now, a baseball program with a 30-count roster can have up to 30 full-ride scholarships.

Also, the NCAA increased some rosters. In one such instance, scholarships for Division I football programs increased from 85 to 105, all full rides. And that doesn't even count the money a collegiate player can now be paid. Obviously, that is a big advantage to wealthier schools and those with a lot of money coming in.

Another thing causing disruption in intercollegiate athletics today is the transfer portal. A student athlete can transfer every year and potentially never have to sit out. The danger for a mid-major D-I program like CBU that has a really good player is another program could come along and offer that player serious money to transfer. It's hard to argue with that. In recent years, CBU has lost players from several teams to other programs through the transfer portal. Some went to Power Four programs, but often the motivation was the money players were given to transfer.

At CBU, we are nimble, and we will do what we can to be competitive. I remember when CBU did not have a nursing program, and then the laws changed in California when Gray Davis was governor. It took about six months to recognize that enough had changed so that nursing would become a more desirable major and would pencil at CBU. So, we started the nursing program and today it is the largest single program that CBU offers. We will handle athletics in much the same way. We are keeping a close eye on the changing landscape in athletics, and we will be very nimble. If there are opportunities, then we will try to take advantage of those. If there are threats, then we will respond accordingly.

Yes, it's a very different era, but we have navigated through many different situations in the past. There is no question that athletics, especially intercollegiate athletics, is going through an inflection point. And one really can't predict how it will all shake out. I don't think anyone could have predicted five years ago, or even three years ago, the situation that exists today. And I think the situation three to five years from now likely could be as different or even more unlike the changes we've seen in the recent past. Whatever happens, we will see how it fits in with CBU and what the role of athletics will be for us in the future.

In the meantime, my takeaway from the pandemic still holds. Whatever happens, we are not going back to the way things were.

Chapter 17

Healthy Tension

In 2025, California Baptist University marks 75 years of providing students "a Christ-centered educational experience that integrates academics with spiritual and social development opportunities." [29] Founded in 1950 by churches in the Los Angeles Southern Baptist Association, CBU continues to honor the original mission statement contained in the institution's 1954 Articles of Incorporation:

> "...to provide training for Baptist youth and others desiring to be affiliated with Baptist theology and theological instruction and such other instruction as may be needful and advantageous in preparing and qualifying ministers and others for Christian work." [30]

CBU focuses on traditional operational issues common to most colleges and universities like accreditation, recruiting, and funding. Unlike secular public and private higher education institutions,

---

[29] calbaptist.edu. "What is CBU's Purpose?" Accessed September 7, 2024. https://calbaptist.edu/about/cbu-at-a-glance/mission.

[30] Ibid

however, CBU approaches these from a decidedly Christian worldview. CBU firmly upholds its historical Southern Baptist identity and conservative Christian values. But doing so in one of the most progressive states in the nation creates inevitable tension. Over the years, we have seen tension rise and fall between the university and the entities it deals with. These include government, culture, society, and even CBU's denomination of origin. Using a proven three-part strategy, however, CBU has been largely successful in avoiding or minimizing conflict. Instead, we see differences as healthy tension to be navigated by identifying core non-negotiable values, anticipating problems, and maintaining open communication.

I think a lot of healthy tension exists because CBU and different entities the institution deals with are moving through space and time at different speeds. For example, many Southern Baptists tend to have a very traditional approach compared to others in the West. It's almost in the DNA of the South, whether you're talking about 1845, 1955, or 2024. If you were to do a spot check at any of those points on the timeline, you would probably rate the traditional approach as positive in some respects but not so good in others. Generally, Southerners are more traditional in how they approach everything from sports to clothing to music. Take country music, for instance; it developed in the rural South, and it tends to honor tradition and the past. Country music is not usually progressive, while pop music often is on the cutting edge, leading the vanguard of social and cultural change.

CBU remains a conservative Christian university in a secular state. California is known for a progressive social and political climate that, in my view, is moving toward hostility to traditional values. If you juxtapose California with the South, California would be seen by most as cutting edge while the South would be noted for a slower-moving, traditional pace, for better or worse.

California's progressivism is rooted in the rich history of the state. After James Marshall discovered gold at John Sutter's sawmill near the town of Coloma in 1848, California became the destination for a certain type of person lured by the "Eureka!" experience that became the state motto. Adventurers who came to be known as

49ers migrated to California from all over the world because they wanted a different life. A better life. They wanted more and were willing to pay a big price for it; they were willing to leave home. Many Southerners were among those trekking to California during the Gold Rush, turning their backs on a familiar, traditional lifestyle and seizing the opportunity to create themselves anew.

For me, that context is important in recognizing CBU for who we are and where we are. It helps explain the reason for the tension. And it helps us focus on trying to make the tension healthy. For example, a number of folks at CBU tend to look at the world from a traditional Baptist and Southern-tinged worldview. Ironically, however, we're doing that in arguably the most dynamic, forward-looking, entrepreneurial fashion. CBU is working to create the future. California dreaming. What are we dreaming about? We're dreaming about Great Commission freedom. We're dreaming about changing the known; not just making sugar water but changing the world.

Today you can come to California and do what? Perhaps more than anything, you can create change. California is not only progressive, but also very influential. When I look at the Golden State, I see some very big trendsetters. First, California is home to Hollywood. The center of the entertainment universe is about 60 miles from the campus of California Baptist University. Just up the coast in Silicon Valley, world changers are inventing the future of the Internet and digital media. Apple, Alphabet/Google, Cisco, Intuit, Oracle, Meta/Facebook, Uber. They're all in California, creating the next new thing and having a global impact that already permeates the culture in California.

And then there is California's higher education sector, dominated by the University of California system. The public UC system arguably is one of the finest research-oriented, cutting-edge, create-tomorrow-today educational systems on the planet. California also is home to some of the nation's premier private institutions, including Stanford University, the California Institute of Technology, and the University of Southern California.

Alongside such behemoths, CBU could be seen as a comparatively small college with traditional values, living in a very exciting, energized, change-the-world environment. To survive and thrive in these conditions, there would need to be what I refer to as healthy tension. That means we would first look at who we are and what our values are. Then we would strip them down until only what is non-negotiable remains. But for CBU to be comprehensive in its academic and extracurricular offerings, the non-negotiables would need to be few. In many respects, the CBU campus culture and environment would be a prototype of the traditional South. So, since we would be doing this in California, the conditions for success may not be present. However, if CBU had no non-negotiables and adopted the California culture progress, it would be unrecognizable in a generation or two. So, that validates the idea of having a healthy tension, recognizing that it's there, and letting it be sort of a framework for how we make decisions at CBU. Understanding how to safeguard conservative values amid overwhelming liberal influences remains an ongoing journey.

I will give you an example. I came to CBU in 1994 and soon recognized we needed a model for how to function as a conservative Christian college in California, a secular state moving toward hostility to traditional values. Such a model was not to be found in, say, Birmingham, Alabama. We were not going to be able to do on the so-called 'Left Coast' what they could do in the Deep South.

What kinds of models are there? I wondered. Where could we find models for how to hold on to core values in an extreme environment? Then in 2004, nearly a decade into my presidency, I found a useful model. Not in California, not in the Deep South, but in the People's Republic of China, of all places. The model was Yanbian University of Science and Technology (YUST).

The story of how YUST came into existence is fascinating. Dr. James Chin-Kyung Kim, a Korean American businessman from Miami, had a vision to create a Christian college in Communist China. He wanted to build it in a semi-autonomous district in China's Jilin Province that is home to a large population of ethnic

Koreans. In the mid-1990s, the region had more inhabitants of Korean extraction than Han Chinese. Situated in the northeast part of China known as Manchuria, the region appealed to Dr. Kim because of its proximity to the Korean Peninsula.

Dr. Kim pursued his vision with dogged determination. He worked tirelessly, raising money and negotiating with the Chinese government. Finally, he received permission to build a campus for a Christian college in the People's Republic of China. Founded in 1992 as "a collaboration of the People's Republic of China and numerous foreign volunteers", YUST was the first Chinese joint-venture university in the Yanbian Autonomous Prefecture and grew to become one of the country's top universities."[31]

Dr. Kim built the campus in Yanji. YUST faculty and leadership administrators are Christians from around the world. Some are supported by a sponsoring evangelical organization. Others are former university educators living on retirement income. The university provides the faculty comfortable housing and meals.

In October 2005, I made the first of several visits to YUST. As I walked around the campus, I noticed there were many restrictions: witnessing about Christ was not allowed and neither was praying in class or in public. YUST was not allowed to display religious symbols, conduct chapel services, or offer academic courses with a Christian focus, like New Testament studies. But as soon as I entered the campus, I sensed the presence of the Lord. Despite severe restrictions imposed by the Chinese Communist Party, that feeling permeated the campus.

At that time, YUST had some 2,200 students and most were Chinese. They were there not because they were Christians, but because that was where they were allowed to go to college.

On a Sunday morning during my visit, I addressed scores of worshippers attending a service held in a former crematorium on the campus. It was a surreal experience. Present for the service were YUST employees from the Netherlands, Australia, Canada, the

---

[31] YUST PUST Foundation. "About YUST." Accessed September 7, 2024. https://yustpust.org/yust/.

United States, the United Kingdom, and other nations. However, no students were allowed to attend. Wow! I thought.

I would spend a lot of time processing the experience to understand more about it. I realized it was part of a personal pilgrimage, a learning experience with me as the observant student, drinking deeply and trying to think it all through. The situation is almost an oxymoron. Here is a conservative Christian college in a communist country. They can't have chapel services. They can't pray in class. They can't witness openly. They can't! They can't! They can't! But even when you strip all that away, the Holy Spirit is still there.

It was a watershed moment for me. When I returned from YUST, I spoke with CBU trustees in an executive session. I said, "We can't be looking at Birmingham, Alabama or the South for an example of how to do conservative Christian college in California. But I've just had this experience in China where there is a conservative Christian college that is thriving!"

Experiencing the way YUST operates in a harshly restrictive environment made me think about the bare minimums for CBU. I began to consider; what things really are non-negotiable at CBU? Some people are called to be outspoken on the topic du jour; whatever is going on today, they are going to speak out. That has never been my style. I take more of a grind it out, work in the vineyard approach. I try to be hospitable and welcoming to others. I focus on being a good neighbor and pursuing excellence across the board; academic programming, campus landscaping, building maintenance, food service, etc.

So, what are the handful of things that are non-negotiable for CBU? If we had to give up chapel, could we figure out another way to worship? I think we could. And we would sing and give honor to God. If CBU were not allowed to teach religion courses, would it still be worth existing? Because of what I experienced at YUST, I began to think, Oh, yes it would! We would find a way.

Then the question became, what am I not willing to do? What is my non-negotiable? The list needs to be very small, so here is what I came up with. If the government of California sent me a letter saying everyone at CBU must worship the governor as a deity, well, that would be blasphemous. I would be willing to die opposing that, and I would be willing to put this university at greatest risk over such a mandate. For almost anything else, however, let us figure out how to continue to operate CBU with fidelity to its mission and values.

That first visit to YUST was a spiritual journey that provided me with a context for how to frame this palpable tension. In the 19 years since then, the trend toward increasing secularism has grown rapidly. In addition to growing more secular, the environment is becoming more hostile to traditional values including faith values.

Sometimes tension can develop with CBU's sponsoring denomination and the way that Southern Baptist polity works. I would say I have been very fortunate, leading an operational entity that is strongly affiliated with the state Baptist convention. There have not been many issues, although occasionally some arise as social change moves more quickly. We have tried to anticipate what these issues would be and mitigate them before they come up. That has served us well.

One such issue came up early in my presidency. In the mid to late '90s, criticism arose over a spike in the number of students with visible body piercings, tattoos, and hair dyed unnatural colors. This was brought up in a study session at a board meeting by a trustee who wanted to know what the administration was going to do about this. I tempered my response with a bit of humor. 'We need to be very careful that we don't overregulate this,' I explained, 'because where I go to church, there are several elderly ladies who have blue hair, and that's certainly not natural." People laughed and the tension was relieved.

What I was asking was, do we really want to go there? We had a thoughtful discussion and talked through the issue. We agreed that society is changing, and that some of us may not particularly care for it. But we managed not to create a regulation dealing with students' body art.

Today it is not uncommon for some Baptist churches in

California and some other states, to have a worship leader or pastor with visible tattoos. That just speaks to the speed at which these changes happen. As a lifelong Southern Baptist, I have seen that Baptists often lag on a lot of social issues, but they do tend to catch up on many of them. Whether that's good or bad, I'm not the judge of that. Society tends to be more cutting edge, while Baptists tend to be more traditional, slower to change. One example in many churches is the trend involving traditional hymns giving way to contemporary worship songs.

Another issue that developed early in my presidency happened when CBU increased its outreach to the adult market. Traditional students are typically 18 to 22 years old, living on campus or commuting. They go to class from 8 am until 2 pm and then have laboratories, intramural sports, and other experiences in the afternoons.

Most non-traditional students are adults who often work from eight to five. Before the advent of distance learning, if you were going to teach non-traditional students, you had to do it in the evenings. But when CBU began offering a mid-week evening class for the adult market, a local Baptist church complained that the schedule conflicted with Wednesday night prayer meeting. We taught out that class and changed the schedule to avoid repeating that conflict. After several years, the pastor who had lodged the complaint moved on to another area. By then, Wednesday evening classes were no longer much of an issue. The tension had passed.

When I became president, CBC was affiliated with the National Association of Intercollegiate Athletics (NAIA). Most of the NAIA member institutions were small colleges around the country. As CBC started growing as an organization and its budget grew, we moved up to NCAA Division II. After a few years there, we moved up to NCAA Division I.

Before the D-I era at CBU, the Lancers did not play games on Sundays. I had a regulation that teams needed prior written approval from the president's office to even practice on Sunday. A typical request would involve one of our teams visiting Hawaii for an away game on Monday. The coach would ask if the team could practice on Sunday afternoon. I would usually say yes, while taking great care to ensure team practices did not interfere with traditional worship time. This was done so student athletes could attend church services, and to avoid criticism from conservative, traditional Southern Baptist churches. To this day, we try not to play games before noon on Sunday; 1 pm is better. Many Baptists still worship primarily on Sunday mornings. However, some of the bigger churches have worship services on Saturday evening and many people choose that service in place of the traditional Sunday worship. Even so, when we're hosting a game on the CBU campus we try to not start games before noon if possible. As we moved into Division I, however, it became difficult to do. Fortunately, there seemed to be more reasons to allow Sunday team practices and games since people could choose to worship at other times. We have taken strides to prevent tension with churches over the issue, and it seems to have worked out well.

When I arrived in November of 1994, CBU did not have a swimming pool on the campus. I felt it was important to have one. So, by 1998 we built an aquatic center and started competing in men's and women's swimming and diving and men's and women's water polo. Leading up to the opening of the pool complex, I took the proactive step to develop a mandatory dress code. This was to ensure proper modesty for those using the aquatic center.

I asked Kent Dacus, the vice president for student services, to organize a committee made up of women and men, staff members and students. They were tasked with researching best practices at other Baptist and evangelical colleges across the country and crafting a dress code for the CBU aquatic center. Most of the work was done by the vice president and administrative staff. They wrote letters, asking, "Do you have an aquatic center? And if so, do you have a dress code for swimming suits? And if so, would you please send us a copy?"

The committee received some responses and then developed a detailed code for CBU. The guidelines included written and pictorial standards that people knew they had to follow at the aquatic center.

Females using the aquatic center had to wear a one-piece swimsuit with specific lines to ensure modesty. We were not saying that there is anything wrong with a two-piece swimsuit, just that if you're swimming in this pool, this is the dress code. The standard for males was board shorts, reaching almost the top of the knee. Speedos were allowed only for men's swim team competitions. The women's swim teams used uniform one-piece swimsuits.

The aquatic center was available for community groups to conduct swimming lessons and recreational activities. Churches occasionally would have their annual picnic at the CBU pool, so we went over the rules with them. The standards applied for everybody using the pool, not just for the CBU community.

When the guidelines were approved by the Board of Trustees, some board members were amused that we had gone to such lengths. But I felt that the issue probably would be a big deal for some people. So, I decided, let's just hit it head on and create a reasonable process. We even went to the lengths of having several approved styles of swimsuits available to buy for a modest price if someone came and did not have the proper swimsuit.

Those are four examples of issues that caused tension for CBU through the years. They may seem minor to some, but each case could have been explosive. Anticipating potentially prickly issues and dealing with them proactively has been an effective approach that has helped reduce tension and avoid conflict.

Many people mistakenly think that CBU is a Southern Baptist institution within a denominational hierarchy. It is not. We do have a very strong affinity and non-binding affiliation with the Southern Baptist Convention. CBU identifies as Southern Baptist by virtue of its origins and values. But it is not a Southern Baptist Convention entity. I sometimes point to the University of California as an example to explain the distinction.

The University of California is a state government institution, created and operated by the State of California. It has many ties to the federal government, such as research funding, but UC is not a United States government entity. The only higher education institutions owned and operated by the United States government are its five service academies. These are: the Military Academy, also known as West Point; the Naval Academy; the Air Force Academy; the Coast Guard Academy, and the Merchant Marine Academy.

In some ways, CBU is like the University of California. UC is operated by the state government in California, one of 50 autonomous states in the union. CBU is an entity of the California Southern Baptist Convention, which relates to the Southern Baptist Convention much like the way a state relates to the federal government. But one is not reporting to the other per se. CBU is operated by California Southern Baptists who elect the Board of Trustees. That's the main relationship. While CBU does not receive a lot of funding from the CSBC, the convention keeps its board control mechanism.

The leadership team at CBU spends a fair amount of time dealing with government entities and accreditation issues. Student financial aid involves two levels of government: the state of California issues Cal Grants for qualifying students; Pell grants, Stafford Loans, student loans, work study funding all comes from the federal government. The U.S. Department of Education establishes and enforces myriad regulations that impact higher education. The California Department of Education is one of several entities that regulate colleges and universities in the state. For example, the California Bureau of Registered Nursing (BRN) is a state agency that CBU deals with often. The BRN oversees nursing education and practice in the state, including Bachelor of Science in Nursing programs like the one at CBU, to ensure they comply with regulatory and statutory requirements.

There are about 1,000 new laws in the state of California every year. I have been here 30 years; that's some 30,000 new laws that CBU (and everyone else in the state) must follow. And that's not counting the ones that are already on the books. It is almost impossible to keep up with all the laws one is responsible for. Obviously, all of them don't affect everyone. But in my opinion, having so many laws, many of them extensive in scope, creates an environment where the government does not have the depth and breadth to enforce them all. Pragmatically then, some laws and regulations are emphasized; they can't all be enforced uniformly. This creates its own moral hazard.

State and federal governments both tend to be consistently more intrusive, regulatory, and prescriptive about how individuals, businesses, and organizations are to conduct themselves. Both sides impose more laws and more regulations. Just expect that it is coming and with it, more control.

Another of CBU's exacting regulatory relationships is with the Western Association of Schools and Colleges (WASC), one of six United States regional accrediting bodies. The WASC Senior College and University Commission (WSCUC) is the quasi-governmental organization that provides umbrella accreditation for CBU. In addition, many programs the university offers receive accreditation from other accrediting bodies.

Athletics at CBU is subject to extensive regulation by the National Collegiate Athletic Association (NCAA) and the Western Athletic Conference (WAC). Several sports at CBU that WAC does not promote relate to other conferences with regulations of their own. Each of these regulatory relationships, governmental, academic, and athletic, is a potential source of tension for CBU. With so much oversight from so many entities, a significant amount of time and energy goes into dotting all the I's and crossing all the T's required to continue operations.

California Baptist University spends quite a bit of time, energy, and financial resources on marketing, recruiting, and ensuring that there is sufficient capacity to teach classes and support student services. It is a large operation, and it requires a lot of heavy lifting to realize and sustain the vision of a university committed to the Great Commission. In all of it, there is a necessary tension as a condition for success.

Looking at life that way and working to prevent or mitigate negative consequences when tension develops helps us stay out of the ditches on the sides of the road. It also keeps us from focusing on just the money or the buildings or the programs, so that we don't forget why we are doing what we do. It keeps us asking, what's different about CBU? What's unique? What is the sacred, spiritual aspect of what we're doing? Like these questions, the element of tension is critically important. Some level of tension is necessary to be healthy and productive, for individuals and organizations alike. But too little or too much tension can create dysfunction. Working to achieve the delicate balance that creates healthy tension has been a constant theme at California Baptist University for the past three decades.

Chapter 18

Building Blocks and Champions

"Building blocks" is a term I use to describe the crucial elements needed to develop a comprehensive university. That's a higher education institution that offers a wide range of majors and academic disciplines and serves various purposes. Successfully developing such an institution requires skillfully combining complementary academic programs, facilities, services, and activities to build up the university. Non-academic areas like athletics, spiritual life, and student housing are other building blocks that also contribute to developing campus culture.

There are three main areas that we emphasize for the large residential population at CBU. First, we looked at spiritual environment as a primary campus culture builder. Next, we wanted an extensive intercollegiate athletic program. Along with that we wanted a strong intramural program to keep students bonded, involved, and excited. Each of these is an integral building block at California Baptist University.

I think of the individual building blocks for a university like pieces in a rock wall; not bricks that are uniform in shape and size, but rocks that all have their own unique sizes and shapes. Stack them in a certain way and they make a very strong, distinctive formation. Combined, they can become something great and truly impactful.

The land and buildings that make up the main campus and physical plant form a crucial building block in the composition of California Baptist University. When I came to CBC, the campus consisted of 59.5 acres. Today, the campus measures about 168 acres. Very few of the buildings on campus were built for the purpose for which they currently are used. For instance, the university has bought several apartment complexes and houses over the years. A number have been converted to non-residential uses, such as offices and administrative space. The historic James Complex, which features some of CBU's main academic buildings, was constructed in the 1920s and 1930s as a Neighbors of Woodcraft (NOW) retirement home. The building that houses the Annie Gabriel Library originally served the NOW retirement home as an infirmary.

Campus buildings constructed by CBU and some conversions are more purposeful. The university bought hundreds of apartment units that were built on our block in the 1970s and turned them into student housing. In addition to enlarging the campus, this also protects the school. If we ever need to go back to market with those apartments, we can. Once you build a dormitory, it's only going to be a dormitory. So, we've tried not to build that kind of single-purpose student housing. For example, CBU's newest student housing facility is Magnolia Crossing.

Magnolia Crossing, built in 2020

The four-story, 540-bed residential complex was brought online in 2020. It features 93 apartments, each with two or three bedrooms, a kitchen, a living area, and two or three bathrooms. Magnolia Crossing was built by design in a way that could easily convert to market rate apartments if that need were to occur. Again, such convertibility helps protect the university.

A key building block that has been a significant part of the university's growth is CBU's spiritual foundation. When I arrived as president, I was pleased to find an impressive chapel program and over the years we have worked to make it even better. Chapel services at CBU feature ministry leaders and nationally acclaimed speakers who inspire students, faculty and staff.

Along with chapel, we have quite an active spiritual life program in CBU residence halls, where Resident Advisors and students can engage in Bible studies, prayer, and spiritual counseling.

The importance of the spiritual foundation at CBU also can be seen in the way we have strengthened the Christian Ministries program. The name itself is more focused than what it replaced. California Baptist College had a religion department, but when the institution became a university, we wanted to heighten its visibility with a name that represents the Christian identity of CBU as a

Baptist institution. And we have further strengthened that identity by adding programs such as the Bachelor of Theology degree and developing a Christian Ministries faculty that is recognized among the finest in the nation.

CBU has also become known for the International Service Projects (ISP) that we began in 1997. ISP has grown as CBU's flagship service program overseen by the Office of Spiritual Life. Each year, hundreds of students take part in two to eight-week cross-cultural service experiences with field partners in locations around the world.

CBU's faith-based higher education experience is woven into the fabric of every academic program that the university offers. Faculty members take part in workshops on integrating faith and learning, both in the orientation of new hires and in refresher sessions for CBU's veteran teaching professionals. The influence of spiritual foundation on CBU academics is manifested through classroom instruction that emphasizes critical thinking with a Christian worldview. This is measured against universal outcomes developed at CBU that are called the Core Four. These outcomes are designed to ensure that students are academically prepared, biblically rooted, globally minded, and equipped to serve.

Arguably, any university's most important building blocks are its academic programs. Unlike a strictly liberal arts college, a comprehensive university may specialize in areas like engineering, sciences, humanities, or social sciences. During my three decades as president, I have led development of California Baptist University into a comprehensive, Christ-centered, private institution that includes all of these disciplines. CBU also has four professional schools, offering programs in business, Christian ministries, education, and nursing. Some of these programs are larger than others, and that's fine; they don't all need to be the same size. The key is that they fit together, and they all complement each other, and they contribute to building the university.

When we look at starting a new academic program at CBU, I categorize it as either a gap program or an impacted program. I'll give you an example of each. A gap program is one where the market is not being serviced. The Inland Empire has gaps in a number of areas. Whether you're talking state judges, hospital beds per capita, or baccalaureate nurses per capita, these are gaps in the market. CBU has the only university architecture program in the Inland Empire, which is defined as Riverside County and San Bernardino County. The two-county region has a population estimated at 4.7 million, larger than 26 states in the union.[32] So, architecture is a gap program. CBU has the only Bachelor of Science in Nursing program on a university campus in Riverside County. That's another gap program. CBU is the only four-year comprehensive university in the region offering a degree in aviation science. These are just a few of the gaps in the marketplace.

An example of an impacted program in our region would be engineering. Seven miles from the CBU campus is the University of California, Riverside, a major research university, with a college of engineering. In the early 2000s, the program had a robust enrollment, and leaders decided not to increase the number of students. They were turning away people who wanted to study engineering.

When I learned that, I thought that CBU could develop its own undergraduate engineering program. I believed that the market would sustain it, and in 2007 CBU launched a school of engineering. In fall 2024, the Gordon and Jill Bourns College of Engineering at CBU enrolled nearly 800 students in an ABET accredited engineering program with 10 majors. These include biomedical engineering, chemical engineering, civil engineering, computer science, construction management, electrical engineering, general engineering, industrial and system engineering, mechanical engineering, and software engineering.

Before 2007, there was a strong engineering program in our city, but it was impacted. Since then, the growth of the engineering program at CBU has proved the market is strong enough to support two such programs in Riverside.

Strong, passionate leaders or "champions" are essential to develop and run new programs. When considering whether to start

[32] US States - Ranked by Population 2024. World Population Review. Retrieved September 14, 2024, from https://worldpopulationreview.com/states

a program, we assess if it would be viable by doing due diligence. This typically includes a market analysis, needs assessment, cost analysis, and business plan. If we feel there is a market for the program and we understand the cost factors, the next key step is finding the champion. This step is so critical that we have delayed starting new programs for up to two years at CBU because we did not yet have the champion.

The champion of a new academic program usually is going to be the founding dean or department chair. In an entrepreneurial organization like California Baptist University, the deans are key to their programs' success. That's because they have the expertise in their respective areas and they're the ones who are running and administering the programs. To me, a champion will be passionate about the program and involved in all aspects of it. The champion who becomes a founding dean is someone who helps to identify all the employees in that area. They're also going to write the curriculum and organize clinical sites that may be involved in the program. They may not be doing these things personally because they're going to have help. But the dean must know all of it in depth. Because any one of these key ingredients that isn't correct, from student recruitment to admission standards to the curriculum to clinical sites to specialized accreditation standards and securing equipment, can hinder or even doom a program to failure.

Consider, for instance, securing and scheduling delivery of equipment for multi-year programs. What kind of equipment will we need to have in place when the first-year students arrive? What will we need for the sophomores, and then for juniors, and then finally for seniors in an undergraduate program? In many cases, it is not necessary to have all the pieces of a four-year program in place from the outset, if a certain lab or equipment is only used by students in their fourth year. Just-in-time scheduling can spread out costs and help start new programs faster.

I consider the way we began engineering at CBU as a model of the right way to start an academic program. Our due diligence indicated that the program would be a differentiator for us. We knew there was sufficient demand to support an engineering program at

CBU, and we determined that it would differentiate the university in the Christian higher education market. So, we decided to move forward and began a national search for a champion.

Dr. Jonathan Parker, CBU's vice president for academic affairs and provost at the time, brought me the promising resumé of an applicant for the position of dean of engineering. After reviewing the resumé, I thought the applicant looked great on paper. But would he hold up? We scheduled him for a campus visit and interview, and when Dr. Anthony Donaldson arrived for the interview, it took barely a minute to see that he would.

Dr. Donaldson is taller than average with a confident, affable manner and engaging smile. When we met for the first time, his appearance suggested an absent-minded professor; his hair looked windblown, his shirt was not quite tucked in. However, I soon understood that he was an excellent fit for CBU. He had a Ph.D. in electrical engineering from Texas Tech University, and a deep personal commitment to the Great Commission.

CBU college of engineering dean Dr. Anthony Donaldson at a dedication event in 2007

After he received his Ph.D., he enrolled at Asbury Seminary, a conservative institution in Wilmore, Kentucky. He earned a master's degree in Missions and Evangelism at Asbury, and then became a tentmaking missionary in India for two years. Tentmaking is a biblical term based on the Apostle Paul, who made tents to pay living expenses and support his ministry of witnessing for Jesus.[33]

Dr. Donaldson said he was frustrated in his current position at a Christian institution in another western state. He explained that he had big plans to grow the engineering department that did not jibe with the plans of the organization in which he was working. So, the idea that he could be a founding dean at a university committed to the Great Commission, and do that in Southern California, was appealing to him. I laid out my vision for an engineering program at CBU, and then Dr. Donaldson described how he would implement his vision within that. Our visions meshed. We were instantly sympatico.

When we decided to offer engineering at CBU, I prayed we would find someone with a Ph.D. who was a good fit to lead the program. We needed a champion who would be passionate about founding the program and committed to the Great Commission. I would tell the champion, "Here are the ditches and here are the resources. You will need to do everything it takes to build this program, and we'll support you with that. You've got to be the one with the vision and the drive to make it succeed. We're giving you the keys; you've got to be the driver."

Anthony Donaldson was the answer to my prayer. He accepted the challenge, came to CBU, and went to work with energetic passion. He championed engineering at CBU for 15 years before stepping down as founding dean of the Gordon and Jill Bourns College of Engineering on June 30, 2021. During his time at CBU, Dr. Donaldson built a tremendous program, growing it into a highly respected college with five ABET-accredited engineering programs. Another degree program in the college, computer science, is also accredited by ABET.

33 Acts 18:1-5

Selecting the champion for a program is critical to help ensure its success and longevity. One example of this approach that continues to yield great results at CBU is the choice of Rick Rowland as founding coach for the aquatics program.

CBU swim and dive coach Rick Rowland looks on as his team practices in the pool

Rowland had been a standout swimmer and water polo player at Pepperdine University. He competed on Pepperdine's water polo and swim teams coached by his father, Rick Rowland, Sr. After graduating from Pepperdine with a bachelor's degree in physical education and kinesiology in 1981, Rick joined his father as an assistant coach for swimming and water polo. Later, he coached and taught classes at Villa Park High School from 1988-93, and then at Santa Margarita High School from 1993-98.

When I arrived in the mid-1990s, CBC was having trouble booking summer camps because there was no swimming pool on campus. That also meant CBC students had no place to swim. I thought, this is Southern California; we need a pool. So, after three successive years of enrollment increases, we broke ground on an aquatics center to address those concerns and facilitate intercollegiate water sports competition.

We hired Rick Rowland as founding coach for all CBU aquatics teams in 1998, the year the pool facilities were completed. He had one year to recruit the teams, order supplies and equipment, and launch the program. He proved to be the champion the program needed. Right off the bat, his Lancer teams were nationally competitive in NAIA swimming and diving events.

For several years, CBU's main water sports rival was Simon Fraser University (SFU), a public institution with nearly 30,000 students in Burnaby, British Columbia, Canada. SFU was much larger than other NAIA institutions, but at the time, the NCAA did not accept foreign universities, even in Canada, to participate.

Rowland led CBU men's water polo team through its first 16 years of existence (1999-2015) and women's water polo through its first eight seasons (2000-2007). In swimming and diving, the men's and women's teams he coached won a combined nine NAIA National Championships and seven conference titles in the Rocky Mountain Athletic Conference. After transitioning to NCAA Division II in 2013-14, nine of Rowland's 10 squads completed top-14 finishes in their division. The men achieved the program's best showing in the NCAA as national runners-up in Division II in 2018. In 2018-19, CBU's first season in its transition to NCAA Division I, the Lancer men took second place in the WAC and at the College Swimming and Diving Coaches of America Association (CSCAA) National Invitational Championship (NIC). The women placed fourth in the WAC and 21st in the NIC.[34]

From the start, Rowland was head coach for men's swimming and diving, women's swimming and diving, men's water polo, and women's water polo. He was good at it and passionate about it. So, when it became time to hire full-time head coaches for the water polo teams, he was resistant. I reassured him that this was not about his ability; it was about competing at a new level and eventually advancing to NCAA Division I, so we needed a 100% full-time

[34] https://cbulancers.com/staff-directory/rick-rowland/49

coach for each team. We hired new coaches, and Rick continued to oversee the teams, but no longer had a (direct) role in coaching them.

The move to Division I involved a four-year transition. We're now in our third year after the transition, our seventh year in D-I, and the CBU aquatic teams are looking very strong. So, once again, Rowland has managed a very good transition for the program.

During Rowland's tenure, CBU aquatics teams have won multiple national championships and conference titles and produced four individual NCAA champions. Rowland has been honored as coach of the year numerous times, and in 2021 he was voted one of the 100 Greatest College Swimming and Diving Coaches of the past 100 years by the CSCAA.

From starting the aquatics program as an instant powerhouse in the NAIA, to guiding the program through smooth transitions into NCAA Division II and Division I, Rick Rowland has been a total class act. His success in building an aquatics program with enduring quality has strengthened athletics as an important building block at California Baptist University. Like the winning Lancer student athletes he has coached through the years, Rick Rowland is a champion.

Chapter 19

On Donors and Endowment

The history of colleges and universities often includes donors whose signature gifts are transformative for an institution. Two examples that come to mind are Duke University and Emory University.

Trinity College became Duke University in Durham, North Carolina a century ago, after the establishment of The Duke Endowment.[35] The philanthropic foundation was created in 1924 by James B. Duke, whose family was instrumental in developing energy production in the Carolinas. The endowment provided the resources for the private university to expand both physically and academically.

Emory College was founded as a liberal arts college by Georgia Methodists in 1836.[36] It became Emory University in 1915 when the college moved to Atlanta, Georgia. The move came after a $1 million gift from Asa Griggs Candler, the founder of The Coca-Cola

[35] The Duke Endowment. "A Life's Work and Legacy." Accessed September 20, 2024. https://100years.dukeendowment.org/duke-family-name

[36] Oxford-Emory.edu. "Oxford College History." Accessed September 20, 2024. https://oxford.emory.edu/life/history_and_traditions.html#:~:text=When%20Methodist%20leaders%20looked%20to,become%20part%20of%20Emory%20University.

Company and brother of Emory University's 10th president, Warren Akin Candler. Fueled by Candler's gift, Emory has grown to become one of the nation's top private research universities.

When I arrived as president in 1994, California Baptist College did not have a significant donor base. There was no one at the level of giving transformative gifts. In 1991, CBC had even sold 15.5 acres for $5.2 million to keep the doors open. The institution occasionally received modest financial gifts from some churches and individuals. The California Southern Baptist Convention had been giving up to 16.4 percent of its annual budget to CBC, which helped pay operational expenses. But when enrollment started to grow in the mid-1990s, this was not enough for needed capital projects, such as buildings, infrastructure, and equipment.

Shortly after I arrived, we took baby steps to address deferred maintenance, which was a serious issue on the campus. I held meetings with a lot of different groups, getting acquainted with the college and the community. Several of these meetings took place in the multi-use James Complex, which was the largest building on campus at the time. Located at the end of the Palm Drive entrance off Magnolia Avenue, it housed administrative offices, admissions, academics, and the cafeteria. It was sturdily built, but it was tired looking. In realtors' parlance, the James Complex had good bones, but it lacked curb appeal because of deferred maintenance.

I shared my vision for CBU with a local citizens committee at a meeting in the Smith Courtyard, an open-air quadrangle inside the James Complex. The group had been raising money for several years, and I had been tipped off that they had $14,000 they wanted to give to CBC to plant a rose garden. I thanked them for their generosity, and then mentioned the importance of curb appeal. I said the building had not been painted in a long time, and it could really use a new coat of paint. Refreshing the exterior would help recruit students and look more pleasant for people driving by or coming to the campus.

When I learned how much money the group planned to donate, Don Evans, our chief business officer at the time, negotiated a bid from a painting company. For $14,000, they would paint the outside of the building, minus the enclosed courtyard. The citizens committee agreed to fund the painting project.

I had been on the job only four or five weeks when CBC received that first gift of my presidency. We wasted no time putting the money to work. When the painting crew completed the job over the 1994 Christmas break, the result was remarkable.

We were planning my inauguration for late spring across campus at the Van Dyne Gym. But there was a big, inconvenient problem; the unpaved parking area next to the gym was a sand lot. When people exited their cars for an event at the gym, their shoes would sink into the sand, particularly ladies wearing high heels. We needed to pave the parking lot but had no money to pay for it. Fortunately for CBC, Ernest Eugene "Gene" Yeager had already been thinking about a gift to do that.

Gene Yeager was a principal at E.L. Yeager Construction Company, one of the largest public works and private construction businesses in the country. The family-owned company built public projects throughout Southern California, including the 15 Freeway, the 91 Freeway, and part of historic Route 66.[37] Yeager Construction earned acclaim and a multi-million-dollar bonus for quickly rebuilding two bridges on Interstate 5 damaged in the 1994 Northridge earthquake.

Gene Yeager's wife, Billie, had attended CBC.

So, Gene went with me and other CBC staff members to the sandy lot outside the Van Dyne Gym. We walked the site and talked about where asphalt, lights, and landscaping might be used to create a nice parking lot in time for the inauguration.

[37] Kitroeff, Natalie. "Jacques S. Yeager, ex-UC regent who led an influential construction firm, dies at 94." Los Angeles Times. April 20, 2026. https://www.latimes.com/local/obituaries/la-me-0421-jacques-yeager-20160421-story.html. Accessed September 20, 2024.

Gene and Billie Yeager at the CBU campus

I had already told my team to let me do the talking. So, as we were going over the plans, I said to Gene, "You know, this has been dirt since Genesis 1," and then I waited. Gene laughed and paused, and then he said, "Here's what I'm going to do. I'm going to write CBC a check for $75,000. Yeager Construction will come out and pave the lot, and you will be billed for $70,000."

I said, "Well, what is the other $5,000 for?"

"Use that for landscaping, incidental costs, whatever you need," he replied.

One of the things I really appreciated about Gene Yeager as a donor was, just about every time he gave money to the school, he over gave. Whatever he pledged, he over gave.

The second time that happened was after I visited the Living Desert Zoo and Gardens with the Yeagers and their close friends Peggy and Jim Wortz. The Yeagers invited me to join them to introduce me to the Wortzes. Peggy, a former CBC trustee, was the granddaughter of R.E. Olds, the inventor and founder of Oldsmobile automobiles. She was a major donor at the Living Desert in Palm Springs, about an hour and a half drive from the campus. We toured the attraction on an extended, eight-passenger golf cart. I was not aware that such machines existed. I remember commenting on how comfortable the vehicle was; I was really impressed.

A week or two later, Gene Yeager was back on campus, and he came by my office. He handed me a single pink sheet from a telephone message pad. On the back, he had written the name and model number of the shuttle vehicle we used on our visit to the Living Desert. He said, "I want you to look up the cost of one of these, the shipping, tax, everything. Get your CBC colors on it, whatever you want, and then let me know how much it is."

I asked Don Evans to track down the information because we didn't have anything like that; it was before the internet. He secured a catalog, we decided the features we wanted, and Don calculated the price with a sales representative over the phone. The total came to something like $9,300 and change. When I gave the price information to Gene Yeager, he said, "That's fine, I'll send you a check." And, of course, the check was for $10,000. Once again, Gene Yeager over gave.

The third example would have arguably the greatest impact of them all on the future development of California Baptist University. One day in 1997, I was home with a 102-degree fever when the telephone rang. Jane answered the call, and told me, "It's Dana Horn and Gene Yeager on the phone." I said, "Okay," and I took the call.

Dana Horn was a former CBC trustee. His wife, Melba, later served on the board that hired me as president. As I put the phone to my ear, Dana said, forcefully, "We've got to get the land back," referring to 15.5 acres CBC had sold six years before.

"Well, that would be great," I agreed. "What are you thinking?"

Dana told me that he and Gene Yeager had talked with Dan Moon about how to get this land back. Moon had helped with the sale to a Korean billionaire in 1991. Now, with a financial crisis eroding wealth across much of Asia, the Korean owner was unloading some of his Southern California real estate holdings at bargain prices.

Dana Horn and Gene Yeager suggested that I offer $3.2 million to buy back the land that CBC had sold for $5.2 million. Horn and Yeager pledged gifts of $100,000 and $500,000, respectively, to help underwrite the transaction, and the Board of Trustees approved the plan to finance the remaining cost.

Dr. Ellis poses with Melba and Dana Horn at the Yeager Center groundbreaking

The gift from Gene Yeager involved a wire transfer of bank stock. The CBC development office didn't have much experience with processing wire transfers, so it took over a week to set it up. By the time we took delivery of the funds, the stock value had grown to $568,000. Gene had pledged $500,000, so I called to see what he wanted to do with the extra $68,000 that CBC had received in the transfer.

When I told him what had happened, Gene laughed and said, "Just keep it and use toward the purchase." Yet again, he over gave.

Dan Moon and I flew to Seoul, Korea to make the offer to buy the land. We met in the owner's oversized top-floor office in the tallest building in Seoul. The Chairman, as he was known, spoke English but when we arrived, he and Moon conversed in Korean as I stood there, looking on. Moon told him that I was authorized to offer $3.2 million for the land. The Chairman, who stood to lose $2 million on the deal, was visibly displeased. The discussion continued, more animated than before and with voices raised, but finally the Chairman agreed to sell at the price I was authorized to offer.

News that we had reacquired the land was enormously well received by our constituency. They had seen the enrollment growth for several years, so things seemed to be headed in the right direction. But this was a concrete example of tangible progress. I used to joke with the board and others that this would become part of our strategic plan: every five years we would sell the land for one price and buy it back for $2 million less!

Shortly after that, in executive session with the board, I received permission to pursue buying up the rest of the block. And over time, we have been largely successful in doing so. Looking back, that probably would not have been possible without the prompting and generosity of two key donors, Dana Horn and Gene Yeager, that led to recovery of the land that had been sold before I came to CBU.

In 2003, we built the Eugene and Billie Yeager Center, the two-story, 100,000-square-foot main administrative and academic building that also houses the Alumni Dining Commons and three other food service locations.

Dr. Ellis and Jane commemorate the groundbreaking of what would become the Eugene and Billie Yeager Center

Dr. Ellis readies for construction of the Eugene and Billie Yeager Center

One wing of the L-shaped complex is named in honor of Dana and Melba Horn. The namings were in recognition of the Yeagers' and the Horns' service and generosity to CBU over many years.

The Yeager Center is the heart of a larger project that also added parking, a beautiful new entrance for the university, and fencing across the front that dramatically transformed the CBU campus.

Ironically, there was no signature gift for what has become a signature building at CBU. We raised some money for the Yeager Center, but we received only a few major gifts, so it was paid for with the university's operational budget and financing. I thought that growing enrollment and erecting new buildings would bring donors out of the woodwork, but they just weren't there.

So, it took a quite a bit of time to receive CBU's first million-dollar gift, not counting cumulative support from the California Southern Baptist Convention. In the 2000s, we raised more than a million dollars from a group called Women of Vision to help start the nursing program at CBU, but that was a collective effort of a number of people.

When major gifts began coming in, they often were designated for academic programs and projects. And often, these were paid in installments over several years. Then things really started cranking when we built the 100,000-square-foot engineering building, which attracted several major gifts. The Gordon and Jill Bourns College of Engineering is named for donors who gave generously to help start the college, with more than $6 million in total gifts to date.

The three-story building that houses the Bourns College of Engineering is named for Dennis and Carol Troesh, who gave the first eight-figure gift that CBU ever received. The Troesh's committed $10 million, paying $2 million annually for five years, like clockwork. Another million-dollar donation for that project came from Bill and Sue Johnson, longtime supporters of CBU. Bill Johnson was key principal of Johnson Machinery Company. Sue Johnson's grandfather, P. Boyd Smith, was founding president of California Baptist University.

Dr. Ellis with Bill and Sue Johnson

The Johnsons and Troeshes previously had given seven-figure gifts toward construction of the Business Building at CBU.

In October 2023, the Business Building was named the Hae and Shina Park Building, honoring the family's gifts to CBU totaling more than $6 million. The Park Building houses the Dr. Robert K. Jabs School of Business, Innovators' Auditorium, and Career Center.

A notable feature that I have seen develop in CBU donor relationships is the meaningful impact that connection has on donors and their families. In some cases, the connection outlives the original donors and continues through their survivors. When Peggy Wortz passed away in February 2008, I received a call from her family who said one of her last wishes was to have her funeral at CBU. We did not hold many funerals on the campus, but if somebody asked, we would try to accommodate their request. We agreed to honor her wish, and a public memorial service for Peggy Wortz was held in the Wallace Theater on March 1, 2008.

Among those who attended the service were Gene and Billie Yeager. Their connection to CBC had begun in the 1980s when Billie attended CBC's adult education program. It grew through the years as they served and gave generously to the university. Gene especially enjoyed the beautiful CBU campus. Sometimes he would visit and admire the buildings and landscape amid the bustling activity of the Stamps Courtyard, just outside the Yeager Center.

One Sunday in early September 2010, Jane and I were leaving Magnolia Baptist Church. As we were walking to our car, I switched on my mobile phone and saw that I had missed a call from Billie Yeager. So, I returned her call and when I told her who I was, she said, "Gene has died. Can you come?" As we spoke, I learned that Billie was with other family members at the Yeager home in Indian Wells. I told Billie that Jane and I needed to stop briefly at our home to get a few things, and then we would be right out.

As we visited that afternoon, Billie said, "Gene really appreciated having Peggy Wortz's funeral on the campus, and he would like to do something similar." I asked if he had wanted his memorial service to be held in the Wallace Theater.

"No, it's not big enough," she replied. I suggested the Van Dyne gym, but Billie thought that wouldn't be appropriate. So, I asked, "Where would you like it to be?"

"He loved that outside courtyard," she said. "Could we have it out there?"

I said, "Absolutely."

The family wanted to hold the service at mid-morning during the week, so we brought in chairs and rented a huge white tent that filled virtually the entire Stamps Courtyard. The celebration of life for Gene Yeager was held in the heart of the CBU academic campus, one of Gene's favorite places, just days after the start of the fall semester. We told students, faculty and staff about the service in advance, and everyone was very respectful.

The service was packed with family, friends, and dignitaries from all over the Inland Empire and beyond. Many knew Gene from his work heading up Yeager Construction's extensive portfolio of public works projects. Others knew him through his many civic, charitable, and religious activities. To CBU, Gene will long be remembered as a dear friend and supporter whose love for the institution and many contributions will have a positive impact on students for generations to come.

Gene and Billie Yeager also played a key part in the university's largest gift to date, when they introduced two of their Coachella Valley neighbors to CBU. Dale and Sarah Ann Fowler divide their time between residences in Massachusetts and Southern California, including a home six doors down the street from the Yeagers in Indian Wells. Dale, an Orange County native, became interested in real estate development early in his career when he was a college student at Chapman University. He was still in his early 20s when he built his first 10-unit apartment complex. Eventually, he pivoted from residential apartments to industrial buildings. Today, the Fowlers' family-run business owns some three million square feet, all of it debt free, with 500,000 square feet dedicated to charity.

The Fowlers have two grandchildren who graduated from CBU. Their earlier gifts to CBU supported endowed and general scholarships and the Endurance Fund, created to help the university through the COVID-19 pandemic. Then in February 2023, the couple gave CBU the largest gift in its history, $28.5 million. In honor of the gift, CBU named the 5,050-seat indoor campus arena the Dale E. and Sarah Ann Fowler Events Center. The facility opened in 2017 and hosts CBU chapel services, Division I basketball games, commencement ceremonies, and other special events.

When I came to CBU, the institution's endowment was about $3.8 million, a very small amount. But we didn't emphasize that with donors, because we needed bricks and mortar as enrollment increases created capacity issues. For many years, when donors said they would like to give an endowment, I would reply, 'That would be fantastic," and then ask them to consider using that money for whatever building project we had going. Most of the time the donor would say, "That will be fine." If a donor insisted on giving an endowment, of course we would accept it, but that did not happen much.

Then, the Great Recession hit, sharpening our focus on growing the university's endowment. The university's cash flow was dependent on an early delivery of Cal Grant funds received in the middle of August. The amount, several million dollars at the time, was based on what the university received the previous year. Once enrollment figures were finalized in the fall, the Cal Grant program would provide another infusion of funds. CBU had set up a line of credit for emergencies but had not used it for a long time. So, the August Cal Grant payment was critical for the university's cash flow.

The recession caused serious problems for the State of California including a protracted budget process in 2009. Without an approved budget, the State could not deliver the August Cal Grant installment but issued a special kind of IOU, called a Registered Warrant, instead. The warrant promised payment later, but that didn't help CBU's cash flow needs. So, we tried to tap the line of credit, but the bank refused to let the university use it because it had been idle for so long.

Strapped for cash, the university almost missed making a payroll that summer. Fortunately, that did not happen, but I decided that would never happen again. CBU was going to build up cash reserves and that would require some significant austerity measures.

I held a campus town hall meeting and announced we were suspending pay raises and limiting university contributions to employee retirement accounts for the next couple of years. I explained that this was needed to create a $5 million cash reserve from operating surplus funds. We thought it would take two years, but after 18 months we were able to resume retirement contributions and pay raises while still building the cash reserve. Long term, our plan was to set aside $5 million a year for five years to protect against financial emergencies. We realized that goal and created a $25 million cash reserve.

At that time, CBU endowment was still anemic, totaling around $18 million and not growing appreciably. I was reviewing financial forms used by tax exempt nonprofit institutions to share information with the public and something caught my eye. I noticed there were different types of endowments. One is a restricted endowment where the principal is held in perpetuity, while earnings from invested assets are spent as specified by the donor. Another is a quasi-endowment, usually started by the institution that benefits from it; the principal is typically retained while earnings are distributed or spent.

I introduced the quasi-endowment concept to the Board of Trustees. After talking it through, the board approved shifting the university's $25 million cash reserve to quasi-endowment. That action boosted CBU's endowment from about $18 million to $43 million but the total changed very little for the next two or three years because we weren't adding to it.

By the middle of the 2010s, CBU was enjoying substantial annual budget surpluses. We thought, what if we took some of that money and used it to match endowment gifts of $25,000 or more? For example, if a donor gave $100,000 to an endowment controlled by CBU, it would instantly double to $200,000. Half a million dollars would become a million dollars. People love leverage, we reasoned, and this might be a way to kickstart endowment growth.

The 2010 California Baptist University Board of Trustees

So, with board approval, we launched the endowment matching plan, and it had the intended effect. As giving increased significantly, so did the endowment fund. This continued happily for several years.

In 2021, Gary McDonald, a major donor from Central California, came to talk with me about the endowment for the School of Christian Ministries. We had lunch with Dr. Chris Morgan, Dean of the School of Christian Ministries; Dr. Chuck Sands, Vice President for Academic Affairs and Provost; and Paul Eldridge, Vice President for University Advancement. I figured McDonald was going to announce a two- or three-million-dollar gift. I knew he really loves the School of Christian Ministries and wants it to thrive. But what he said took me and everyone in the room by surprise.

"I have a $40-million proposal," McDonald said. "I propose giving $10 million to the school over five years, to be matched by other donors." A donor would give, say, a million dollars and McDonald would make it $2 million. Then he added another layer: he wanted to know if CBU would match both of those gifts, effectively increasing the $1 million gift to $4 million?

I said the plan would have to be approved by the board, but I felt sure they would. And they did. We started the CBU portion of the match from operational surplus. So, when a donor gave $250,000, it became a million-dollar endowment controlled by the university for the School of Christian Ministries.

Wow! The concept was explosive. CBU had already done a one-to-one endowment match with great results. Now, donors were getting a three-to-one match, and the idea caught fire. The five-year, $40 million endowment challenge was so powerful and so well received, that in September 2024 we announced that it was fully subscribed, one and a half years ahead of schedule.[38] With

[38] calbaptist.edu. "California Baptist University reaches its $40-million endowment challenge ahead of schedule." Accessed September 22, 2024. https://calbaptist.edu/about/news-events/news/california_baptist_university_reaches_its_40_million_endowment_challenge_ahead_of_schedule.

the success of that challenge, the School of Christian Ministries endowment had grown to some $60 million.

The focus on endowment growth has dramatically increased donations received by CBU. In the last several years, we have raised about $20 million a year; in one year, gifts totaled nearly $44 million. That may not be that much for some institutions, but for California Baptist University it is a healthy number. And I see that continuing in the years ahead.

The impact of focusing on CBU endowment growth has been remarkable. Endowment grew from less than $4 million in 1994, to about $18 million in 2010. The quasi-endowment plan approved by the board re-designated CBU's $25 million cash reserve, more than doubling endowment to $43 million in the mid-2010s. Endowment matching programs and other gifts have since increased CBU endowment to $168 million. And as we continue efforts in this area, achieving a $200 million endowment looks increasingly within reach. Ideally, a university the size of CBU should have much more than that, but we are building momentum and moving in the right direction.

Chapter 20

Global Impact and Tales from the Trail

I came to California Baptist College in 1994 with a vision to transform it into "a university committed to the Great Commission." Four years later the institution became California Baptist University, and we were on our way to realizing the vision. But there was more to building a university than just changing the name, and more to the vision than what was said explicitly in those seven words.

The Great Commission is a key tenet of Christian theology that emphasizes evangelism, baptism, missionary work, and ministry. The specific instructions, or commission, that Jesus gave to his disciples are recorded in the Bible in Matthew 28:19–20. The Great Commission confers three main commands; to go, make disciples, and teach. So, as I envision a university committed to sharing the mission of Christ, I imagine something greater than a finite physical campus in Southern California, or anywhere, can contain. From the beginning, I envisioned CBU as a university committed to the Great Commission *with a global impact for Christ*. So, one of the questions I asked myself was, how are we going to actualize that?

Using the opportunity planning technique discussed earlier, I was constantly looking for opportunities to present themselves. In 1995, I had the idea of starting International Service Projects to actualize what the Great Commission teaches. I chose the program's name intentionally. First, the program would be international in scope. By design, participants would 'go' to other countries. Second, the program would focus on service, in keeping with the ministry aspect of the Great Commission. Third, the program would be project oriented and purposeful. Hence the name, International Service Projects, or ISPs.

Students and others who take part in ISPs raise funds to pay for the service and learning experience. That includes travel and food expenses for the project. And the hosts, individuals or groups that ISP teams work with are not charged anything for the team's service. That way, teams are not a burden on their hosts.

ISP teams typically train for two semesters before their projects, which usually are conducted during summer. At first, the projects lasted about three weeks. Now, options up to 10 weeks are available for those considering mission vocations after graduating. Most teams consist of eight students and two chaperones, often faculty members or university staff. Each team partners with individuals or groups in the destination country to help with needs named by the host group.

Many teams partner with missionaries sponsored by the International Mission Board of the Southern Baptist Convention. Our first preference would be a career IMB missionary who graduated from CBU. After that, we try to work alongside other IMB field personnel or other types of affinity missionaries, ideally with a tie to CBU.

ISP team projects often are suggested when the host missionary or agency provides a list of needs. We review the lists and decide if there is something a team has the ability and the interest and the competence to do. And on a typical 21-day ISP trip, there's usually no more than two or three days of sightseeing. This is not tourism; this is about going and doing a service project. ISP projects have included digging water wells, conducting vacation Bible schools and sports camps, and working with refugees, orphanages, and medical clinics. Often, ISP teams work with English as a Second Language (ESL) students. These are for people who want to practice speaking English with North Americans to learn accents and idioms that English speakers from other regions often do not have.

Sometimes an International Service Project will develop another way. Several years ago, a CBU engineering student went to Mexico with her church group and came across a battered women's shelter that had no clean running water. The student talked with one of her engineering professors and a return visit to the shelter was made to assess the need. Then, with the professor overseeing their work, CBU engineering students designed a water filtration system. They raised money, procured all the materials they needed, and then returned to the shelter and installed the system.

Before the start of International Service Projects, in my first year as president, something happened that would expand my horizons and enhance future CBU opportunities for Great Commission impact. Dr. C. B "Bill" Hogue was the executive secretary of the California Southern Baptist Convention and had been a key member on the CBC president search committee. He was one of the three wise men who came east to visit my wife and me in Campbellsville, Kentucky during the search process. He was also deeply involved with the Baptist World Alliance (BWA) as the North American vice president and member of the General Council, the organization's governing board. As an officer, he would recommend people to serve on various BWA committees, commissions, and study groups. So, shortly after I arrived at CBC, he started working on me to go to Buenos Aires, Argentina in August 1995 to attend the BWA World Congress.

Bill would call me every month or so and say he wanted to nominate me for one group or another, and I would reply, "Well, let me pray about it." During one of the calls, I said, "Look, I'm so focused on getting ready for the new semester and closing out the previous year. I don't really have the money or the time to do this. It's my first year here (at CBC), so I really would prefer to wait."

Still, he wouldn't take "no" for an answer. After several months of this back and forth, Bill insisted that I agree to go to the BWA World Congress because he had to send in the names. So, I said "Okay." I studied the calendar, and I figured the longest I could afford to be away from campus for the event would be five days. That would give me a day to travel to Buenos Aires, another to return, and three days at the congress in between.

I don't remember how I paid for the plane ticket, and there wasn't even money for a hotel room. But Mark Wyatt, then editor of the *California Southern Baptist* newspaper, had a room with his son at the headquarters hotel. They let me crash with them; Matthew took the sofa without complaining so I could have one of the beds during my abbreviated stay.

I made the trip to Argentina reluctantly because I was so focused on enrollment and everything that needed to be done at CBC. But it was a tremendous experience for me because it opened my eyes to the greater Baptist work being done around the globe. Thousands of Baptists from all over the world were at the congress. I'm an observant guy, and I quickly understood that it really was about the Great Commission. I perceived this was an opportunity CBC could seize to begin to do things on the world stage.

For the next 15 years, Mark Wyatt and I became frequent travel partners, attending BWA gatherings and managing CBU connections and relationships worldwide. We attended three of the next four Baptist World Congress meetings: Melbourne, Australia in 2000; Birmingham, England in 2005; and Durban, South Africa with my younger son, Erik, in 2015; plus, nearly all the annual General Council meetings in between. We literally have seen the world together, from South Africa to North Korea, and many other countries on six continents. On our travels it would not be unusual for us to visit other places along the way, such as historical Christian sites and noteworthy architectural treasures in different parts of the world. I'm big on colleges, so I would explore universities new and old to learn from their designs and gain inspiration for the ongoing development of CBU.

Once, while traveling in the Middle East, Mark and I made a

quick side trip to Istanbul, Türkiye, to meet up with an ISP team in the field. We arranged our visit to coincide with the team's day off, so we could enjoy a meal together and learn about their experiences without interfering with their service project. Before leaving, we stopped for a group photo in front of the historic Hagia Sophia Grand Mosque, built in the sixth century as the main Byzantine Christian church in ancient Constantinople and converted to a mosque by the conquering Ottoman Empire in the 15th century.

Before the side trip to Istanbul, Mark and I had been in Lebanon where I was the commencement speaker for the Beirut Baptist Academy.

Dr. Ellis and Dr. Wyatt in Lebanon

I had been invited by Dr. Nabil Costa, a Baptist leader in the region and Executive Director for the Lebanese Society for Educational and Social Development (LSESD). After meeting at a BWA meeting some years before, we developed a partnership between CBU and LSESD. It included a modest student exchange program and training conferences conducted at the Arab Baptist Seminary in Beirut and led by CBU professors.

Lebanon's recent history included military conflict and occupations involving two neighboring countries. There had been a protracted Lebanese civil war and armed hostility continued between opposing militias. When we arrived in the Lebanese capital, the rubble of war still littered parts of the city. Dr. Costa took us to a restaurant in the country's famed Bekaa Valley, where tanks and armored vehicles at strategic locations stood ready for action as reminders of the ongoing tension. It was especially unnerving to see sandbags and barbed wire machine gun emplacements at the entrance of the hotel where we stayed in Beirut.

The commencement ceremony for Beirut Baptist Academy was held in the evening in an open courtyard at the school surrounded by high-rise buildings. The school was undamaged by the Scud missiles that had rained down on Beirut. The academy's exterior walls were free of bullet pockmarks that were visible in parts of the city. Given the region's recent history and continuing violence, however, concerns about safety and the risks inherent in the outdoor setting seemed reasonable. But we learned that Hezbollah, the Lebanese Shia Islamist political party and paramilitary group, had put the word out that the school was not to be touched. More than 90 percent of the students at the school were from Arab families, and Beirut Baptist Academy was considered a sanctuary for students of all faiths; not just the majority Muslim population, but Christians and Jews as well. And so, the commencement ceremony took place without incident as the graduates and their families celebrated a significant life event.

My involvement with the Baptist World Alliance was eye-opening in many ways. I met people from all walks of Baptist life, laypeople and leaders alike, including Dr. Costa in Lebanon. I also became better acquainted with David Maddox, a longtime donor of the university, and his close friend, legendary South Korean pastor Billy Kim. A former BWA president, Kim is the founder of the Far East Broadcasting Company. He shot to fame as a young man, serving as interpreter for American evangelist Billy Graham's crusade in Seoul where a million people were in attendance. I have enjoyed getting to know Billy Kim well over the years and count him as a dear friend.

Along with his storied career as a crusade evangelist, Dr. Billy Graham was active in global Christian organizations such as the Baptist World Alliance. He and his ministry also were instrumental in founding the Internet Evangelism Coalition, Christianity Today Magazine, and the Lausanne Committee for World Evangelization. The latter is known today as the Lausanne Movement, and for several years CBU has been actualizing the Great Commission as a participant of this organization. Dr. Matthew Niermann, associate dean of CBU's College of Architecture, Visual Arts and Design, has served several roles in the Lausanne Movement since 2010. Most recently, he has been director of the State of the Great Commission Report for the Fourth Lausanne Congress held in September 2024 in Incheon, South Korea.

The Lausanne Movement has a program to help emerging Christian leaders around the world earn graduate degrees. Dr. Niermann connected CBU with this Lausanne program, and currently 12 of these future leaders are enrolled in the university's online programs. Half are pursuing master's degrees, and the other half are in doctoral programs. CBU pays tuition for these students with donated funds, and the students or their sponsoring entities buy their books and supplies. Several students have already earned graduate degrees at CBU through this program. However, since many of them are from other countries and completed their degree work online, few have visited the CBU campus, and it is rare for one to attend commencement. So, I was excited to meet with some of these alumni and students at an event celebrating CBU program participants during the Fourth Lausanne Congress in South Korea.

Developing future leaders has been a keen interest and passion of mine throughout my presidency at CBU. Some students rise above the crowd, displaying exceptional ability and potential. I take special interest in this kind of talent and enjoy helping them develop as leaders. Three special examples come to mind.

Mikko Sivonen, a native of Finland, came to CBU to play volleyball as a student athlete. He arrived at CBU as an unbeliever, but he started dating one of our women's track athletes who was a very strong Christian. Through her influence, Mikko became a believer. After earning his bachelor's degree, he enrolled at Golden Gate Baptist Theological Seminary (now Gateway Seminary), and I lost touch with him. We reconnected when Mikko was chosen as a graduate assistant to work with the search committee that recommended Dr. Jeff Iorg to become president of the seminary. I was a member of an advisory group involved with the presidential search process, so after that Mikko and I stayed in contact.

Mikko earned two master's degrees at Golden Gate Seminary, then enrolled in a ThD program at the University of Helsinki. After earning his doctorate, he serves under the auspices of the Southern Baptist Convention's International Mission Board (IMB) as a pastor, and as a lecturer in Biblical Studies and academic dean of Agricola Theological Seminary in Finland. Every few years, Mikko, his wife, Heidi, and their five children spend a semester at CBU, where he is a guest lecturer in the School of Christian Ministries. It also gives the children an opportunity to reconnect with Heidi's side of the family in Southern California.

Recently, Dr. Iorg retired as president of Gateway Seminary to become the eighth President and CEO of the Southern Baptist Convention Executive Committee. During the search for his successor, a friend asked me if I had a recommendation. I told him about a globalist I know who is a Gateway Seminary graduate, a pastor, and a seminary dean. I mentioned some international programs that currently are doing well for Gateway, in Singapore and elsewhere in Asia, and then I connected the dots.

"You probably don't need anybody from the South to be the next Gateway president," I said. "But you may want to consider somebody from the southern part of Finland."

Gateway Seminary trustees selected Dr. Adam Groza, a long-time associate of Dr. Iorg, to succeed him as president, an excellent choice. Dr. Mikko Sivonen continues to serve with the IMB in Finland. A former Lancer with a definite up arrow, Mikko has more than confirmed my belief in his leadership abilities.

Yukai Sun is another CBU graduate I stayed in touch with long after he graduated. A native of Shanghai, China, he had been attending Fudan University, one of the top 50 universities in that country. He transferred to CBU on a volleyball scholarship and enjoyed success on the court and in the classroom. Yukai also became a believer while at CBU, and later attended Moody Bible Institute.

In the summer of 2006, Mark Wyatt and I attended a student recruiting fair in Qingdao, China where a dozen other Southern Baptist affiliated colleges and universities also were showcased. The competition for students was stiff, but we had a secret weapon: a 6'4" charismatic, winsome, Chinese-born, Mandarin-speaking CBU student athlete, Yukai Sun. After setting up the booth, Mark and I stepped away and let Yukai do the talking. He was a rock star! Prospective students lined up and looked up, since Yukai was head and shoulders taller than many of those attending the recruiting fair.

We passed through Shanghai on our return to California, and Yukai proudly showed us his hometown and introduced us to some truly memorable Chinese dining. Yukai was a business major at CBU; now he works for a private investment firm that invests in family-owned or owner-operated companies.

Dr. Ellis speaking at a university in China

Lucas Wehner came to CBU from the Black Forest region of southern Germany. Enthusiastic doesn't begin to describe Lucas or his love for CBU. Throughout his college career at CBU—he earned bachelor's and master's degrees in business administration—Lucas showed an entrepreneurial spirit and untiring, energetic drive. As a student, Lucas was already seeking ways to connect his alma mater with colleges and universities in his homeland, which complemented CBU's Great Commission values and programming. After graduating, Lucas returned to Germany where he continues to represent CBU as a proud Lancer graduate.

In 2018, Lucas helped arrange and host a meeting that I attended with Mark Wyatt and executive leaders of the Internationale Hochschule Liebenzell (IHL), to explore a partnership opportunity between our institutions. Lucas serves as an administrator in the International and Mobility Office of IHL, a Christian college in

Bad Liebenzell, the heart of a German religious movement known as the Liebenzeller Mission. He has served many years as an officer in the German army both on active duty and in the reserves.

The stories of these three international students are like those of countless other CBU alumni, foreign and domestic. Years after graduating, it is immensely satisfying to see how much CBU meant to them and still does, and how they are raising families, pursuing careers, serving the Lord, and living their purpose.

Much of the international travel I have done as president of CBU has involved exploring and developing partnerships with institutions of higher education in other countries. I get opportunities to present at conferences and sometimes include partnership development activities on the same trip. Normally when we had an opportunity to partner with a university in another country, Mark Wyatt would go with me. Sometimes others from CBU with specific expertise could also go, depending on what the institution we would be visiting wanted to develop.

One such instance happened early in my presidency on a visit to China, and Dr. James Lu was in the delegation from CBU. Dr. Lu is originally from Shandong, an eastern Chinese province on the Yellow Sea. He has a Ph.D. in English Literature from Duke University, but Mandarin is his native language. So, he served effectively as our interpreter on that trip. I am reminded of that trip often while sitting in my office, because a document from the visit harks back to a special service that Dr. Lu performed.

It was China in 1997, and things were different than now. We were negotiating an exchange partnership with a university and needed to sign a cooperation agreement. But their computer printer was malfunctioning and there was no backup. We had our copy of the document printed in English, but they could not prepare the Chinese version. So, that evening James Lu translated it into Mandarin and wrote it out by hand, so the signing ceremony could take place as planned the next morning. Framed copies of that agreement in both languages are displayed on my office wall. When Dr. Lu retired in 2024, I recalled the special service he had performed and said he would forever be an important part of the Great Commission history of California Baptist University.

Agreements from other Chinese institutions are also displayed on the wall along with one from an evangelical Russian university. Sometimes the partnerships authorized by these documents work out and sometimes they don't. These relationships develop to serve different purposes that usually benefit both institutions. But a common reason for many of the foreign institutions is that their people want to come to America, especially their faculty who want to take a sabbatical. We have arranged quite a few such visits over the years. We provide campus housing and give them an office so they can research and study.

Having international faculty teach at CBU during sabbaticals hasn't worked out very well because of language barriers and the need to ensure that academic standards are being met. More often, the visitors speak in classes or serve as guest lecturers. The student exchange part of the international accords has proven difficult to realize. We have occasionally had some foreign exchange students come to CBU, but the partnerships have produced mixed results. And Americans who want to do a semester abroad tend to prefer popular locations in Europe, so that has limited the scope of student exchanges with institutions in other places.

Still, along with ISP and other programs housed in the Office of Spiritual Life, CBU academics has also grown in global impact and involvement. In addition to semester study abroad opportunities, many regular CBU programs include international travel and learning components. For instance, tuition for graduate students in the MBA program includes a global business trip with fellow students and faculty members. Similarly, students in CBU's architecture program take part in a five-week international trip to Italy. They live in apartments in Florence and Rome, take guided tours, sketch architectural masterpieces, and learn about design, history, and urbanism. In many academic disciplines, international learning experiences help students develop a global perspective, gain professional skills, and grow personally.

Finding ways to actualize the Great Commission has resulted in some interesting and impactful relationships between California Baptist University and educational partners in other nations. Several are worth noting, including Russia, Rwanda, and perhaps most surprisingly, North Korea.

An agreement between CBU and an evangelical university in the northern Russia city of St. Petersburg did not pan out the way it was planned. Instead, it produced a different result with Great Commission impact. In July 2010, Dr. Alexander Negrov came to my office to formalize an Agreement for Academic Cooperation between CBU and St. Petersburg Christian University (SPbCU), where he served as president. The pact authorized plans for faculty and student exchange programs and other cooperative activities. Three months later, in October, Dr. Negrov welcomed me and Mark Wyatt to the SPbCU campus in St. Petersburg, where I spoke at a chapel service, toured the facilities, and learned about the challenges of running a Christian higher education institution in an authoritarian state. During our visit, Dr. Negrov and his wife, Zena, graciously welcomed us for a home-cooked dinner at their modest high-rise apartment. We were excited to see the agreement between our universities take shape and discussed next steps to advance the relationship. But unforeseen events would soon scuttle our plans.

Just after New Year's Day in 2011, I received word from Dr. Negrov that his board had suspended plans to expand undergraduate offerings at SPbCU beyond its limited existing program of theology and ministry training. He said the board had authorized him to take a sabbatical leave and asked him to continue to lead SPbCU in the future.

Dr. Negrov had expressed an interest in the MBA program at CBU and a Ph.D. in leadership studies that we were developing. So, I invited Alex and Zena to CBU for his sabbatical and they accepted. We met together several times and discussed the turnaround I had led at CBU, and he picked my brain about a wide range of topics including higher education, strategic planning, and leadership.

Before his sabbatical at CBU, an unexpected development in

Russia effectively ended Dr. Negrov's presidency at SPbCU. Russian President Vladimir Putin returned to power in 2012 and signed a law requiring anyone receiving support from outside of Russia to register as a foreign agent. The law constrained NGOs and restricted their leadership by foreigners. Because Dr. Negrov was born in Ukraine and had developed a donor base for SPbCU in the United States and Canada, he could no longer serve as its president. So, he used his time at CBU to retool and develop plans for the next chapter of his ministry. Today, he is the CEO and founder of Hodos Institute in Washington State. Hodos (ὁδός in Greek) means path or way, or journey. The mission of Hodos Institute is to partner "with those who are committed to connecting ethical values with best practices in personal and organizational leadership across all sectors of society."[39]

Arguably CBU's single most impactful global Great Commission partnership began developing in the early 2000s after I saw a TIME Magazine cover story about the PEACE Plan developed by Saddleback Community Church. Rick Warren, founding pastor of Saddleback Church, and his wife, Kay, met while they were both students at California Baptist College.

Alumnus Dr. Rick Warren receives the inaugural Presidential Medal of Merit Award from Dr. Ellis

[39] hodosinstitute.com. "Our work: research, training, and consulting." Accessed September 25, 2024. https://www.hodosinstitute.com/work/.

Dr. Ellis, Dr. Rick Warren and Dr. Mark Wyatt

The TIME article was about their work to combat AIDS in Africa through the PEACE Plan, which was designed to Promote reconciliation, Equip servant leaders, Assist the poor, Care for the sick, and Educate the next generation.

Rick Warren's best-selling book, The Purpose Driven Life, had caught the attention of Paul Kagame, the president of Rwanda, a small country in East Africa decimated by a 100-day tribal genocide in 1994. Kagame asked Warren to help implement the PEACE Plan in Rwanda to recreate it as a Purpose Driven nation.

The TIME article caught my eye; the Educate part of the PEACE Plan looked like a natural tie-in for a Great Commission university. CBU developed a special ISP program to conduct ethnographic surveys to help inventory resources in Rwanda. The country had suffered so much loss that the government didn't know what resources still existed in many villages. Our program would send 10 teams of 10 people, one to each of the country's 10 provinces. We called it "10:10:10 Rwanda." We had fewer than 100 participants for the Rwanda ISPs in 2006, but the teams gathered valuable data for the rebuilding effort in Rwanda.

We also learned that Rwanda was partnering with colleges and universities to help educate Rwandan students until the country's schools and colleges could reopen. That sounded like something CBU could get behind.

In 2007, I joined Rick Warren at a Saddleback worship service where we signed a document making CBU the first university to join the PEACE coalition. Rick agreed to introduce CBU to Kagame and he did so at a meeting with him the next month in Rwanda. The Rwandan president agreed to meet with me whenever I could visit him in Kigali. In the meantime, Rick Warren continued promoting CBU as a full partner in the PEACE coalition with government ministers and others.

In October 2007, I traveled to Kigali, Rwanda with Mark Wyatt, and we met with President Kagame and his education minister. Our discussion paved the way for the Rwanda-California Baptist University Presidential Education Agreement. Under the agreement, CBU would provide up to 20 full tuition scholarships for high quality students from Rwanda for four years of study in academic disciplines desired by that country. Most of these would be in the sciences and medical fields. Rwanda agreed to provide travel, room and board, and other expenses for its citizens who qualified for the program. After graduating, the students would be obligated to return to Rwanda for at least five years to help in the nation's rebuilding efforts.

For several years, CBU welcomed new cohorts of first-year students from Rwanda into the program each fall. I was concerned the first semester because at that time the students' native tongue was Swahili, education in their home country was taught in French, and they would be competing in English with students at CBU. Happily, it turned out not to be a problem. Their GPAs (grade point averages) were off the charts, averaging close to 3.9.

At the high point of the program, we had as many as 55 students from Rwanda enrolled at CBU, some in each of the four classes; freshman, sophomore, junior, and senior. All of them were outstanding students. Eventually, the agreement wound down when the government of Rwanda decided to end the program and invest in their own universities that were back up and running again.

Impermanence is a fundamental aspect of life, so the Rwanda-CBU Presidential Education program was bound to end. When it was done, we recognized it as a wonderful learning experience, particularly for the students who benefited from it, and from CBU's commitment to the Great Commission.

Perhaps CBU's most unexpected global connection to date was the result of our partnership with the Yanbian University of Science and Technology (YUST) that began in 2005 and is discussed in an earlier chapter. It included a vibrant exchange, with some of their students coming to CBU to study, and students and faculty from CBU going to the YUST campus in the Chinese region of Manchuria. I made two or three trips to YUST during the most active years of the partnership.

Dr. Ellis with the CBU delegation visiting YUST in Manchuria

Then, leaders of YUST received an invitation from the North Korean government to build a similar university in Pyongyang, the first privately funded university ever allowed in the Democratic People's Republic of Korea.

And they did.

Because of CBU's relationship with YUST I was invited, as was Mark Wyatt, to be part of the foreign delegation at the dedication of Pyongyang University of Science and Technology (PUST). Our visit to the North Korean capital in 2009 was surreal. When we flew into the Democratic People's Republic of Korea from a gateway city in neighboring China, our passports were collected and not returned until after we left the country several days later. We were under constant surveillance during our entire stay in the so-called Hermit Kingdom. The government-run hotel where visitors for the dedication were staying was garishly luxurious compared to average North Korean living conditions. Perhaps not surprisingly, the hotel had few if any other guests.

The PUST dedication ceremony was attended by scores of North Korean officials and some 200 invited representatives of foreign universities, many of us because of ties with YUST. One of the foreign delegates was Dr. Chuck Sands, associate dean of education and professional studies at Samford University, a Baptist institution in Birmingham, Alabama. Mark and I were introduced to Dr. Sands before the dedication ceremony began. We hit it off right away. Chuck told us he had grown up in South Korea as a child of IMB missionary parents; his father was a medical missionary at a university in South Korea and, at times, in China.

Within a year after that meeting in Pyongyang, Dr. Chuck Sands would become founding dean of the College of Health Science at CBU. Five years later, he became CBU's vice president for academic affairs and provost.

Dr. Sands speaks fluent Korean, which has been helpful during his time at CBU since we have made close to a dozen trips to South Korea and probably the same number to China.

On another trip, another year, to another continent, I experienced divine providence in a way I doubt I will ever forget. And there were witnesses; that's right, Mark Wyatt was there, and so was my younger son, Erik. We were traveling to the Baptist World Alliance 21st Congress in Durban, South Africa in July 2015. The trek from Southern California to South Africa is one of the most arduous, taxing, tiring, time-consuming journeys I have ever endured. Just reading the itinerary is tiring. The first leg of the trip was a direct flight from LAX to Brussels, Belgium, where we spent the night. The next morning, we boarded another non-stop flight bound for Johannesburg, South Africa. There was another overnight connection. Finally, after the second night in transit, we climbed into a regional puddle jumper for the final leg of the trip into Durban.

It was a long trip, so by the time we arrived at Johannesburg, we were pretty much out of it. It was late at night, and we were beyond travel weary. It was a struggle just to wrestle our luggage from the baggage claim to the curb outside the terminal, much less keep up with our carry-on items. I had all my valuable possessions in a backpack: plane tickets, passport, my wallet, driver's license, credit cards, cash, everything was in my backpack.

We piled into a taxi and the cab driver pulled out of the airport. I gave the driver the address of the hotel where we would be staying and sat back for the ride. After a while, we pulled off the road and drove through an open gate into the enclosed courtyard in front of the hotel. Ominously, there was an armed guard at the gate and razor wire atop the walls that surrounded the property. We piled out of the taxi, collected our suitcases from the trunk, paid the fare, and went to the reception desk to check in for the night.

As I stepped up to the desk, I looked around for my backpack to retrieve my wallet, but the backpack was nowhere to be found. When I saw that the taxi had already left, I went instantly from drowsiness to major anxiety. I thought about what was now missing and began making a mental checklist of what I needed to do. I hardly slept that night, wondering, "Why is this happening? I am usually very good at keeping track of things, especially valuables and essential items. Now, I don't even have an I.D."

Our flight to Durban was scheduled early the next morning. Considering the late hour that we had arrived at the hotel, it wasn't a long night. We called for a taxi to take us to the airport, and on the way, I thought, "I can't even get on the plane. I don't have a ticket." I figured I would be spending some time at the airport to begin the process of replacing the missing travel documents, starting with my passport.

Johannesburg's O.R. Tambo International Airport has two main terminals: Terminal A for international flights and Terminal B for domestic flights. Arriving at the airport, we drove past Terminal A since we were scheduled on a flight that would begin and end in South Africa. As we drove slowly past the terminal, I saw another taxi stopped at the curb. The driver was bent over, getting a piece of luggage out of the car for the passenger he had brought to the airport. When he stood up, I couldn't believe my eyes. I nearly shouted, "Mark, that's the cab driver from last night, isn't it?"

It was. I asked our driver to pull over and stop, and I got out and walked up to the waiting cabbie. He recognized me from the night before and smiled. And when he said he had my backpack, I wanted to hug him!

He told me he hadn't noticed the backpack in the dark last night but discovered it in the morning light. He was planning to turn it in to the airport's lost and found office when he finished with his fare. Somehow, we spotted him before he could. Everything I had packed in the bag was still there. It was all intact, and we still had time to make our flight. I thanked the driver profusely and asked his name as I gave him a generous tip. He said his name was Moses.

Of course, his name was Moses; what else could it have been? When he handed over my backpack, Moses delivered me from my worst travel experience ever, and I felt overwhelmed with God's providence. The promise of Philippians 4:6-7 flashed to mind:

> Be anxious for nothing, but in everything by prayer and supplication, with thanksgiving, let your requests be made known to God; and the peace of God, which surpasses all understanding, will guard your hearts and minds through Christ Jesus.

If you look up "God thing" in the dictionary you won't find this story, although, to me, it fits the definition perfectly. But if anyone ever asks me to relate a "God thing" that I have experienced, this 'Amazing Grace' account of my backpack—that once was lost but now is found—will be high on the list.

In this chapter I've said a lot about the many places around the world that my role as CBU president has taken me in the past 30 years. I am not complaining about all the travel, even the occasional inconveniences and annoyances that are a normal part of the experience. It comes with the territory, and I recognize it's a privilege that many people do not have. And in a sense, it's an act of obedience; after all, the Great Commission begins with "go."

Chapter 21

Four Presidencies, One Institution

November 1, 2024 marked the 30-year anniversary of my tenure as president of California Baptist University. My first official day on the job was November 1, 1994, and I completed 30 years on October 31, 2024. The next day, year 31 began. It's a technical distinction but it's also a matter of perspective; the view from any milestone is different gazing ahead than it is peering back.

Milestones provide opportunities to pause and take stock, evaluate progress, recognize achievements, celebrate successes, reassess goals, adjust course if needed, and regroup for the next part of the journey. I spend most of my time and energy looking ahead. I can't always see the next dangerous curve or suspension-wrecking pothole in the road, but I have a better chance to negotiate such hazards when I keep my eyes on the road ahead. For me, the same principle applies whether I am driving a vehicle or running a university. In both cases, I will use a milestone to pause briefly at a vista point on the side of the road, reflect on where I was, and return my focus to the road ahead. Thirty years at CBU is such a milestone.

For the past several years, I have often said I am in my fourth presidency at California Baptist University. That may sound nonsensical since CBU is the first and only institution I have served as chief executive officer with the title of president. It was called California Baptist College when I arrived, then changed names in 1998 when it met the requirements to become a university. But it is still the same institution that was founded in 1950 by churches in the Los Angeles Southern Baptist Association. It occupies the same campus it moved to over the Christmas holidays in late 1954, albeit with a much-enlarged footprint today. In a legal sense, CBU is the same Nonprofit Religious Benefit Corporation named in Articles of Incorporation filed with the California Secretary of State.

But while it is the same institution, CBU is significantly different today than when I first arrived. Indeed, growing a struggling private college from 808 students to a robust comprehensive Christian university with nearly 12,000 students has made the institution vastly more complex. Growing the budget from $11 million to nearly $400 million has involved layers and layers of change.

It did not happen overnight; 30 years is a long time. The change happened in stages that developed at different paces and had different durations. Each stage brought new challenges that required new and different resources, skills, and leadership styles. I recognized this a few years into my presidency and have been reminded periodically as each new stage emerged from what preceded it. Oh, and spoiler alert: what preceded one presidency wasn't always another one.

Many things overlapped as CBU transitioned from one stage to the next during my administration. But I can point to four distinct periods within my 30 years (and counting) at the helm. I view these periods as four presidencies at one institution. The First Presidency was the turnaround stage, which spanned the years from 1994 to 1998. The Second Presidency, from 1998 to 2003, focused on building capacity for CBU. The Third Presidency, from 2003 to 2020, was the sustaining growth stage.

The Fourth Presidency should have come next, but its start was delayed for longer than two years by the global COVID-19 pandemic. The stage I call the Pandemic Interregnum began in 2020. When it ended is debatable; either 2022 or 2023, depending on when this state of emergency was lifted or that set of restrictions was relaxed. Whenever it ended officially, what occurred between my third and fourth presidency at one institution severely disrupted operations and altered progress.

I began my Fourth Presidency at CBU as restrictive mandates imposed during the pandemic started to unwind in 2022. This is the current stage, and it is focused on growing stability for the institution. I see this stage continuing into the foreseeable future as the next enrollment goal is determined, new plans unfold, and California Baptist University continues to progress and mature. Before gazing into the future, however, a brief look back at each stage in the 30-year journey so far.

I was a graduate student in the early 1980s when I sensed my calling in life was to become president of a struggling Baptist college and turn it around. By late 1994, I had begun work as president of California Baptist College, and it was on. CBC had 808 students, an $11.3 million operating budget, and a projected $834,000 deficit in the current fund. Deferred maintenance was a serious issue. There was no donor base to speak of and precious little endowment. We needed to get spending under control to have any hope of balancing the budget. And since the college generated revenue primarily from tuition and fees, the obvious way to increase operating funds was to enroll more paying students.

When I was hired as president at CBC, I brought years of theory and practical experience to the job. I had a PhD in Higher Education Administration and had held administrative positions at colleges and universities in Texas, Louisiana and Kentucky. So, I was confident that we could increase enrollment quickly. Failure was not an option. I predicted that we would boost the number of students to one thousand the next fall, a forecast that was met with mixed reactions. When fall 1995 enrollment soared to 1,226, I knew we were on the right track. But there was much still to be done.

Years earlier I had read the autobiography of John Wooden, the legendary UCLA basketball coach. In *They Call Me Coach*, Wooden writes about starting his first team practice every year by teaching new players how to put their socks on properly to prevent blisters on their feet.[40] The proper way to put a sock on doesn't create a crease, so it doesn't cause a blister. Coach Wooden taught all the players he coached that there was a proper way to do things, the UCLA way.

For me, a key takeaway of that lesson is always to start with the basics. I thought, wow that is insightful. When I came to CBC, I thought we needed something similar. We had a lot of good people, but they had not really been trained in the basics or exposed to best practices. It was no knock on them. Coach Wooden had been talking to the best players in the whole nation, and yet he was going back to the basics. So, when I began, I spent a lot of time doing what people might call micromanaging. But I was making sure that each one of these processes was done in a certain way.

Because of my background as Executive Vice President at Campbellsville College, when I came to CBC, I had already developed the Ron Ellis way to do most everything. We had devised some very strong practices at Campbellsville. I went to a lot of seminars and visited other institutions to learn about their best practices. I would bring back what I learned and adapt it to our situation. And because I had such extensive experience at multiple institutions, I understood how a lot of things were supposed to work optimally.

Another technique I introduced at CBC dated back to my days as registrar at Louisiana College. I instructed employees to carry a small notepad that would fit in a pocket, and to make notes about problems or issues that arose during registration or whatever process they were performing. Later, we would discuss the notes and any changes that might be needed to refine the process for the next time. It was a way to instill the idea and practice of continuous improvement.

It took about three years to turn the school around from being in a desperate survival mode to the point that we no longer had to sweat payrolls or accounts payable. During those three years, we didn't add to the faculty. We didn't add any acreage, buildings, offices,

[40] Wooden, John, and Tobin, Jack. *They Call Me Coach.* Waco, Texas: Word Books, 1972.

classrooms, or much of anything. We worked those three years on turning our financial picture around, and we did it by carefully managing expenses and increasing enrollment. In the first year we went up nearly 52%, from 808 students to 1,226. A year later we increased to 1,687, and the year after that enrollment rose to 2,009. We were clearly over the hump and on the way.

That first year we had suspended pay raises and counted virtually every penny to bring the budget under control while working hard to increase enrollment. In September 1995, after my first 10 months as president and a nearly 52 percent enrollment increase, I received board approval to give everyone who was employed on that day a 10% pay raise. The board approved 8% pay increases each of the next two years as the enrollment growth continued.

When I arrived, employees were getting their pay raises at a different time of the year. I decided that would change; the board would approve pay raises based on enrollment. This was another way to focus everyone and demonstrate that CBC was enrollment driven. Enrollment drove the institution's budget. Even today, it drives CBU's budget. In fact, enrollment drives the budgets of most schools in America. Public schools typically are formula funded; that's another way of saying enrollment driven. Very few institutions have enough endowment and third-party pay to not be concerned about enrollment. Regardless of what people think, higher education is an enrollment driven industry.

That First Presidency, in my opinion, lasted three years. We had done it. We were thriving at that point, and we could invest in new programming. The turnaround was accomplished. I began to think about how I would continue to add value to the organization, because it no longer needed to turn around. I did a lot of thinking about this and realized some of the things that I needed to change. I could just be a guy who goes into struggling colleges (and there's never going to be a lack of that) and turn them around. But that's too hard and too taxing on one's emotional and physical health. It's tough to do that. Moreover, CBC became California Baptist University in 1998, adding layers of complexity—and potential— to the operation and to my job. What I was doing had worked for CBC. However, I decided that to continue to add value to CBU, I needed to do this job differently for the benefit of the institution.

My Second Presidency at CBU began out of necessity. In the first three years, enrollment grew to 2,009 students and we ran out of capacity. When I came, there were empty parking spaces, empty beds in residence halls, empty seats in classrooms, and empty offices. Excess capacity allowed us to realize tremendous increases in the number of students we enrolled. Then, suddenly, everything was full. So, we entered stage two, which lasted from fall 1998 to 2003.

We had become accustomed to growth, and CBU was still enrollment driven so there was no decision to stop growing. But now we were not able to grow because there was no longer excess capacity. There was no extra parking, no empty beds in the dorms, no empty seats in classrooms, and no unused office space. It's not that we didn't do anything during this new stage, but it was a very difficult period for me because I'm a growth guy who favors an upward trend instead of flat enrollment.

We would spend the next five years doing things that almost no one would see happening. These projects were under the surface and behind the wall, but they were very important to bring elements of university infrastructure up to date and make it ready for the next phase of growth that would come. During this stage, we upgraded technology systems and facilities. For example, we replaced an antiquated telephone system, which enabled us to install a modern computer system. We addressed deferred maintenance. The campus had plumbing from the 1920s that may not have been the best when it was new, so we spent big dollars for repairs and upgrades. It was a similar story for roofs and other needs that had been put off because there was not enough money to fix things. So, as we were building capacity during this stage, we included as many of these upgrades as we could.

When I arrived as president, much of the nearly 60-acre campus had to be watered by hand because there were not many sprinklers installed. Campus maintenance crews used long hoses with attached sprinkler heads at the end. Other hoses were designed with holes along the entire length to spray the immediate area with water. In both cases, the hoses had to be moved by hand every 45 minutes or so. That meant the crew had to stop whatever they were doing and go reposition the hoses for proper coverage. Doing it this way was labor intensive and inefficient. We needed to install sprinklers to water the green spaces on campus.

An important way we added capacity during this stage was by acquiring adjacent properties and enhancing student housing. In 1998, CBU purchased the Lambeth House, Pine Creek Villas, and Willow Wood Apartments. The Lambeth House has served many uses through the years. It housed the president's office and other administrative spaces during construction of the Yeager Center. After that, it became the administrative center for the CBU School of Nursing.

Robert and Phoebe Lambeth cut the ribbon at the official opening of the Lambeth House

We renovated the Pine Creek Villas and Willow Wood Apartments and converted them into student housing. In 2003, they were collectively renamed University Place Apartments.

In addition to developing new student housing, we worked on upgrading what we already had. One impactful project involved Lancer Arms, four two-story buildings that housed married students. Our priority is to provide housing for traditional, single students, so enrollment growth had left little room for married students in Lancer Arms. But after their first year, many traditional students are not required to live on campus. Even with married students, occupancy levels at Lancer Arms dipped to 65%.

We conducted focus groups among some of the people who had moved off campus. When we asked what would have kept them in Lancer Arms, their answers were enlightening. They mentioned things like screen doors, blinds on the windows, updated appliances, and ceiling fans.

Kent Dacus, vice president for enrollment and student services, handles student housing, so we began to set aside money in the budget each year to address the concerns. Upgrading one building a year, it took four years to complete the Lancer Arms project. In addition to refreshing the openings, adding ceiling fans, and replacing appliances, we painted the buildings. And as each building's renovation was completed, it filled up.

The critical step to repurchase 15.5 acres that had been sold before I became president was completed in 1997. The importance of this action, described in an earlier chapter, cannot be overstated, as it would directly impact construction of the transformative Yeager Center. This, in turn, would usher in the next stage and an unprecedented run of annual enrollment gains.

Early in my presidency, with annual budgets in the low eight figures, we were unable to fix or replace dated, sometimes antiquated equipment and facilities. By the time we reached the next level, however, there was more flexibility to make upgrades. During the second stage we also could hire people with the skill set to run and maintain new systems, and then resource them to achieve higher productivity. Those who had been on the journey had to keep up because we were in a continuous improvement model. There was a culture of change, so I needed people who could grow with the institution. We could train those who have the passion and the ability to grow. But from the outset, I told prospective employees, "If you are looking for a place to build a nest, this is not it. We're all about accomplishing the mission and we're a growth institution."

During the capacity building stage, we continued to study the market and plan new programs that made sense. When an opportunity arose, we always asked, can we put that together with excellence in a way that will pencil? And when we could make it work, we did it.

Capacity limits slowed growth dramatically during this period; fall enrollment dropped slightly in 1999 and 2000. But those would be the only two years of enrollment loss during my three decades as president to date. CBU had several off-campus sites for adult education during this period, which helped keep overall enrollment relatively stable. But running programs at multiple locations stretched us. The lack of space and other resources that limited growth, particularly in the traditional enrollment market, also stimulated creative use of campus facilities. CBU's Evening College program brought a lot of working adults to the campus for classes at night. Even with the addition of new buildings in recent years, CBU is arguably one of the leading higher education institutions in the country in terms of academic square footage utilization. When I began working on my doctorate in 1981, Texas A&M University was growing at a very rapid pace. A&M was a leader in space utilization, and I learned the methods they used to optimize use of limited facilities. I emulated some of those methods at CBU to help ease the space crunch. Even today, we have some laboratories and classrooms that are used starting at seven in the morning and some that are used until 10 at night. Some labs are also used on Saturday mornings. Not only does this help students with their schedules, but it also is a big cost savings for the university. It is far more efficient than using laboratories only three or four hours a day, four or five days a week.

STEM programs that CBU offers today such as those in the health sciences and engineering produce tremendous demand for laboratories. Not everyone can schedule their lab sessions at one or two o'clock in the afternoon. But many who are enrolled in high demand programs will take those labs whenever they can. Scheduling labs at night and on weekends offers convenience for students. Those types of efficiencies also allow the university to not overbuild.

Increasing utilization of limited facilities was one of the measures that helped build capacity during the five-year period that I consider my Second Presidency at one institution. We were getting ready to resume growing the university by building human resources, upgrading technology, and addressing a large amount of deferred maintenance. We began acquiring adjacent properties with the goal of buying up the entire block. Combined, these tactics and actions laid the groundwork that would see California Baptist University become one of the fastest growing universities in the nation in the years that followed.

The start of my Third Presidency at CBU coincided with the opening of the Eugene and Billie Yeager Center in the fall of 2003. The beautiful 100,000-square-foot administrative and academic complex added classrooms, office space, and dining facilities that not only enhanced the experience for current students but enabled an unprecedented influx of new enrollments. We had been building capacity for just that purpose, and in 2003 CBU began a remarkable 16-year stretch of incredible enrollment growth. Ironically, during this stage characterized by sustaining growth, our biggest issue would be keeping up with capacity needs. But that is the best problem any business or nonprofit can have.

Along with the new facilities, CBU came up with a new vision for the university's growth during this period. John C. Funk, chair of the Board of Trustees, challenged me to reimagine the future of CBU, and after studying the matter for six months, I presented a plan to expand program offerings in an emerging family of academic disciplines known collectively as STEM; science, technology, engineering, and mathematics. The plan included an ambitious goal for enrollment growth that would more than double the number of students at CBU. We called it 8080 by 2020, signifying the goal to reach a sustained enrollment of 8,080 students by the year 2020.

Achieving that goal would represent a ten-fold increase compared to enrollment when I arrived as president in 1994. It would require an average net increase of more than 350 students, not to mention continuing to expand capacity, each year until 2020.

Fueled by STEM programs including nursing, engineering, aviation science, and a growing number of allied health offerings, enrollment growth exploded, even posting a net increase of 1,113 students in a single year after three consecutive years of 600-plus gains. In fall 2015, CBU enrollment reached 8,406 students, surpassing the 8080 by 2020 goal five years ahead of schedule. A new enrollment goal was set, 12,000 by 2025, and growth continued increasing steadily, tallying an exceptional 24 consecutive years of enrollment growth. By fall 2024, official enrollment was just 69 students shy of the goal, virtually ensuring it would be reached or exceeded the next fall.

Campus expansion continued in this phase with more acquisitions and new construction helping keep pace with increasing the numbers of students. CBU purchased the Royal Rose and Rose Garden Apartments, the Woodmen of the World building, Adams Villas Apartments, College View Apartments, Magnolia Hacienda Apartments, and Adams Plaza shopping center. The 304-unit Parkside Village Apartments, purchased in 2011, was renamed as The Colony at CBU, adding nearly 16 acres and over a thousand beds to the university's housing stock. Two separate phases of The Cottages student housing were completed a year apart, creating a popular student housing option near the academic core of the campus.

New campus buildings also were erected to house certain programs, provide needed learning space for others, and increase recreational opportunities for the CBU community. The JoAnn Hawkins music building was completed in 2005. The Business Building, now called the Hae and Shina Park Building, was dedicated in 2012. A year later, the three-story Recreation Center was dedicated. In 2014, CBU dedicated the School of Nursing Annex and Prayer Garden. In 2015, construction began on the 5,050 seat

CBU Events Center; it was dedicated in 2017 and later renamed as the Dale E. and Sarah Ann Fowler Events Center.

(from left) Women's basketball head coach Jarrod Olson, senior vice president for enrollment and student services Kent Dacus, Dr. Ellis, vice president for athletics Dr. Micah Parker, and men's basketball head coach Rick Croy standing in front of the CBU Events Center during the grand opening event

The mounted Lancer statue that stands at the entrance of the Dale E. and Sarah Ann Fowler Events Center

The year 2015 also saw the opening of the College of Health Science campus. In 2016, construction began on the 100,000 square foot Dennis and Carol Troesh Engineering Building to house the Gordon and Jill Bourns College of Engineering. It opened in fall 2018. The next year, CBU dedicated the East Parking Structure with more than 1,450 parking spaces and opened the new main campus entrance on Adams Street.

My Third Presidency also featured a sea change in CBU athletics, with the move from the National Association of Intercollegiate Athletics to the National Collegiate Athletic Association (NCAA) Division II starting in 2010. In 2013, CBU became a full member of D-II, competing in the Pacific West Conference. In 2017, CBU announced its acceptance into the Western Athletic Conference and transition to NCAA Division I membership. The transition and D-I competition began the next year. In 2022, after a four-year transition, CBU became a full member of the premier intercollegiate athletics organization in the nation.

The third stage of my presidency was not without challenges and setbacks. On two separate occasions years apart, gathering clouds signaled stormy times ahead, not just for CBU, but for the nation and the world.

The first was in January 2008 when I attended meetings of two higher education groups in Washington, D.C. At those sessions I was troubled by grim reports that foreshadowed what would become known as the Great Recession. I returned from the meetings and called a special board meeting where trustees approved my recommendation to suspend a major construction project that was nearly ready to break ground later that spring. The decision cost CBU $1 million that already had been spent to design the project that was scheduled to break ground later that spring. But cancelling the combination dormitory-parking structure project likely prevented far greater losses that could have totaled many times as much. This cloud contained an unexpected benefit; it helped expedite CBU's acquisition of the Parkview Apartments complex next to the campus, which would be repurposed as student housing now called The Colony.

The Great Recession slowed the rate of enrollment increase at CBU for two years. In 2009 we posted a net gain of just 92 students, the third lowest year-over-year increase in that decade. However, the following year enrollment rebounded with an increase of 610 students, and we resumed years of record-setting growth that continued throughout the 2010s. In fact, we prepared the university's 2020-21 budget based on an expected 700 FTE increase in the fall of 2020. We were so confident about the enrollment growth outlook that we were preparing to open a new four-story residence hall with 540 beds. This would put us at nearly 3,400 beds on campus, and we had deposits on all of them. The future looked bright.

The years of my Third Presidency, from 2003 to 2020, were years of sustaining growth at California Baptist University. This stage was anchored by new signature facilities, expanded academic offerings focused on STEM programs, continuous enrollment growth, and global impact. The impact of an unforeseen global pandemic, however, would slam the brakes on years of progress and development and delay the start of my Fourth Presidency at one institution. In early 2020, clouds began gathering once again but no one could have imagined the storm that would engulf the globe, killing millions and causing disruptions worldwide.

In March 2020, I was in Las Vegas attending the Western Athletic Conference (WAC) basketball tournament. My wife, Jane, was visiting with family in Louisiana and planning to join me. We had tickets to see Shania Twain in concert after the WAC tournament ended. But with the spreading COVID-19 pandemic already starting to impact public gatherings around the country, conference officials were debating how to manage crowds at the tournament.

The presidents and athletic directors of WAC institutions were meeting with the conference commissioner and his staff in a crowded room, trying to work through how to ensure safety for everyone involved with the tournament. Dr. Micah Parker, CBU's athletic director, and I listened to the energized discussion about who could attend, how many people would be allowed in the arena, and what times the games would be played,

If I had to pick a moment when my Third Presidency ended, it was about to happen. Throughout the room, phones start lighting up, ringing and beeping with incoming calls and text messages. The Big Ten Conference had just canceled its tournament. Everyone in the room looked at each other as if in shock. The discussion resumed, but it was more subdued. Within minutes, new calls and messages announced that Southeastern Conference leaders had canceled the SEC tournament. Moments later, another major conference followed suit. Very quickly, the conversation in the room shifted from how to run the WAC tournament to whether it would be held at all. With almost no discussion, the decision to cancel the tournament was made unanimously.

I went back to my hotel room for about an hour and watched the news and then drove out to the airport to pick up Jane. After deplaning, she asked me how things were going. I told her we should get something to eat and then see what's going on. When we got back to the room, we learned that businesses and public places were closing. Las Vegas was shutting down. I looked on the internet to check the seating capacity for the venue where we were going to see Shania Twain. I found out it was over 4,000 and I thought, "Man, we can't go there and sit in that crowd with this all going on." I told Jane, "I think we need to get up in the morning, eat breakfast, and drive home." And that's what we did.

I returned home to find California was shutting down. I remember discussing the situation with my vice presidents in an executive council meeting. No one had a crystal ball, saying, here's what's likely to happen. But it soon became clear: they were going to shut the state down. In my opinion, that is when my Third Presidency ended.

What followed was not my Fourth Presidency, as one would expect in normal circumstances. I did not feel the way I had always felt as president, that I was leading the charge, so to speak. I felt like I no longer had control. Someone else was calling the shots and instead of leading, I had to wait for a non-elected person to decide what we could do at CBU, down to very minute details.

The World Health Organization declared COVID-19 a global pandemic on March 11, 2020. Two days later, a national emergency was declared to combat the spread of the deadly virus in the United States. On March 17, 2020, a lockdown order was imposed in California due to a high number of coronavirus cases.

A week after the pandemic declaration, I felt like I lacked the authority to make necessary decisions for the wellbeing of the university. That had been co-opted by the shutdown of the state, essentially by fiat of the governor. I call the ensuing phase the Pandemic Interregnum, to describe the time between the service of one leader and that of another, even though I was the CBU leader on both sides of the pandemic.[41] That's because from 2020 to 2022, I felt like someone else was in charge, making decisions affecting the institution I was responsible for leading.

Another term I use to describe this two-year phase is COVID Captivity, because of the lockdowns and other enormously disruptive mandates that seemed, at times, arbitrary and capricious.

When the California lockdown was ordered, we were already deeply involved in planning for the fall semester at California Baptist University. We needed to know what restrictions there would be for classes, food service, and student housing. The higher education sector was told that we would have an answer by mid-June. That was getting late, I thought, but maybe we could make it work. But the mid-June delivery date came and went, and there was no announcement.

We asked our representatives at the Association of Independent California Colleges and Universities (AICCU) to tell the governor's office that we needed to know the regulations. We held Zoom video meetings with an aide from the governor's office to no avail. We went all the way through July and there was still no guidance. Time was running out. If you know anything about higher education,

[41] "interregnum." *Merriam-Webster.com.* 2024. https://merriam-webster.com (30 September 2024).

a university is more like an aircraft carrier than a Jet Ski. An institution with almost 10,000 students doesn't turn on a dime. CBU's Magnolia Crossing student housing project took three years of planning, fundraising, financing, and building to complete. We didn't just snap our fingers to make it happen. In the fall of 2020, we were finally ready to move students in and a lot was dependent on those students living there. It was sometime in August when we finally received guidance from the governor's office allowing only one occupant per room in student housing.

What? The majority of CBU's student housing is designed and built for double occupancy. We have some that are singles, but the edict that comes from the governor's office mandates all singles. We had been strategizing and planning how to mitigate the risks by installing shielding to keep two to a room. But there was no discussion, no way to challenge the order.

So, we were going to be able to accept about 1,825 students instead of 3,400. As a result, nearly 400 students who were planning to come in the fall decided not to come at all. They would either take a gap year, go to another college, or do something else altogether. And so instead of having the 700 additional paying students that we were expecting, we would end up seeing only 272. It really hit us hard and as we rolled into the new academic year, it was very stressful.

It had already been a very stressful summer for me. From the time I was a child, I had pretty much been able to use pressure to enhance performance. For example, think of a child shooting hoops in the back yard all by himself. He imagines there are five seconds left in the game, his team is trailing by two points, and as the clock ticks down he takes the shot and nails the three-point buzzer beater to win the game. Even in an imaginary contest, he used that pressure to enhance his performance. Similarly, I've always been able to use pressure and harness it in that way to enhance performance. But the pandemic was different. I still had the feeling of tremendous responsibility, which I had accepted as president of CBU, and I liked it. But I did not like the idea that while I continued to have responsibility for more than 10,000 students, 1,000 full-time employees, 1,500 part-time employees, and a $300 million budget, I was unable to utilize my expertise and my experience. Instead, I was having to listen to an elected official making decisions that did not seem to be in sync with the reality of what was happening on the ground. That was very stressful for me.

As the fall semester got underway, I was still experiencing a lot of stress. It wasn't what I would consider positive pressure that I could channel constructively; I felt stress, and stress is negative. It happens when you feel like you're not in control, and there's no way to harness it or release it. Consequently, I was under a load of stress. In November of that year, I was scheduled for an angioplasty to improve blood flow to my heart and relieve chest pain. But once the medical team saw my test results, they said, "You need to spend the night. You'll be one of the first ones to get a double bypass tomorrow."

After my double bypass surgery, we were working remotely a lot of the time. Essential workers still reported for work on campus and followed guidelines on social distancing. We delivered classes in person, online, and in hybrid mode. We installed clear barriers to separate workspaces and keep people apart. But more and more, the regulations felt arbitrary and unnecessary. I remember a television news report from Los Angeles where a restaurant could only have so many chairs at tables, and they had to keep a minimum distance between customers. Even on the sidewalk outside they were carefully measuring distances to conform with the regulations, which sharply limited the number of customers they could serve. The news media was showing that there was an exception to the strict food service regulations for the film industry. A movie was being shot nearby and the film company catering tent was operating with no restrictions right across the street from the restaurant.

One of the tragedies of the shutdown was that it seemed like for the first time in the history of the country, when faced with a tragedy, the government limited the ability of talented people to handle the situation. I could not recall another instance in history where the government had done this. For example, during World

War II, it was 'all hands on deck.' Everyone was expected to be part of the war effort. Business, industry, and individuals joined with the government in a shared commitment to win the war.

This time was different. I was never asked by government leaders in Riverside County, Sacramento, or Washington, D.C, 'What do you think we should do?' We were ready to help but we were being told to stand down, basically to do nothing. In my view, that was a real failure of leadership.

A representative from one California university served on an advisory panel for Governor Gavin Newsom. Instead of seeking input from other higher education leaders, she simply recited the governor's direction. It looked like we had a seat at the table, when we should have had a table of our own. I was more than 30 years into my career, so I had seen a lot and done a lot. In the pandemic, however, I had to wait for somebody who probably had never worked in higher education to make rules that did not make a lot of sense in every situation. One rule might work in some places, but it's probably not going to work across the state of California.

Some people on campus strongly favored the nth degree of precaution. And there were others who believed it was all kind of ridiculous. My job was trying to keep everything together while having little say in matters because we were waiting for the next word to come down from federal, state, or local officials. For that reason, the pandemic interregnum was the hardest time I've had during the past 30 years.

The relaxation of COVID-19 regulations as pandemic concerns eased in the summer of 2022 became the unofficial line of demarcation that signaled the end of the pandemic interregnum and the beginning of my Fourth Presidency. The current stage emerged in fall 2022, even though the governor's emergency order officially remained in effect until February 28, 2023.

Unlike the earlier stages, the Fourth Presidency is defining itself. The First Presidency was very clear. I knew what needed to be done. CBU was in survival mode. We had to turn it around. We started strong and accomplished the turnaround in three years. The

Second Presidency developed because we were out of capacity, so we had to spend time putting things in place to provide the space and systems needed for growth. That took five years. The Yeager Center and University Place were key steps in that process. The Third Presidency was a tremendous 16-year run of growth and progress, campus expansion, program development, and stabilization that just seemed to go on and on. It only stopped when the pandemic arrived.

As the new stage unfolds, we are focus on regaining institutional momentum that was lost or slowed down during the pandemic. But unlike conditions before the pandemic, it involves adjusting to slower growth in California and higher education. The environment has changed significantly and CBU, like many organizations, is working to adapt to the inconstant conditions. Three examples of these tumultuous times are California's changing population, the shrinking consumer base for higher education, and demographic shifts.

The U.S. Constitution mandates a census every 10 years to count every person living in the United States. The census is used for many purposes, such as determining how to distribute seats in the House of Representatives. California became the 31st state on September 9, 1850, and has been included in the census for 17 cycles. For 160 years, continuing population growth in the Golden State resulted in a gain of at least one congressional seat for California and sometimes more than one after each census through 2010. That changed in 2020, when California lost one seat in the U.S. House.

From 1850 to 2010, California was in an almost continuous growth mode. It may have taken a dip here and there, but it was mostly grow, grow, grow. Now, not so much, and it started before the pandemic. When California lost a congressional district, it wasn't because the state had stopped growing. It was because the rate of growth in California was slower than other places in the national average. Some of the areas that grew at higher percentages got congressional seats.

California historically has attracted residents from across the country and around the world. The number of international immigrants moving into the state reduced sharply during the pandemic, but the inflow from other countries is rebounding. In recent years, however, outmigration from California is exceeding the number of people moving into the state. More people are leaving California for other states than the other direction, which historically has not been the case.

The number of students enrolled in higher education is also a moving target. According to the National Center for Education Statistics (NCES), undergraduate enrollment dropped 15% during the 2010s and continued falling during the pandemic.[42] That translates to millions fewer college and university students than before. While undergraduate enrollment is forecast to increase through 2031, the higher education market remains volatile.

There's a significant amount of demographic change and most of it doesn't seem to be positive. So, for an institution like California Baptist University that is focused on growth, sustaining growth is going to be much more difficult. One thing I have been talking to the board about as we move into this Fourth Presidency is that we are not likely to see those halcyon days of growth that we've experienced in past years.

The good news is that California Baptist University is a significant size for a faith-based institution. With nearly 12,000 students, it is one of the largest private Christian post-secondary institutions in the nation. Remember, we thought 8,080 would be a good number. Today we are basically 50% larger than that. And there's a lot of depth at CBU. We started our first doctoral program in 2015. Today, we have nine doctoral programs with a combined 600 students enrolled. CBU is a very different, thriving institution. During this Fourth Presidency, we are focusing on maturing the institution and increasing stability, sinking roots deep to provide a strong foundation and preserve what has been built.

I have told the board that it is conceivable that four or five years from now, we could have basically the same enrollment overall as

---

[42] National Center for Education Statistics. n.d. "Fast Facts: Enrollment (98)." https://nces.ed.gov/fastfacts/display.asp?id=98.

now, but with a very different mix internally. For example, I could see our graduate market growing robustly. But I don't sense that we're going to have a breakout in the online market, where we currently have about 2,500 students enrolled. That's probably a good number for us. Many of those students know the institution because they're in our service area, and I think that will continue.

CBU's traditional undergraduate enrollment is about 6,700. That's a good number that creates a lot of positive activity and good vibes on campus. Another 3,500 or so are graduate students, including those who are online. Probably 2,500 graduate students are doing their programs on campus and 1,000 are online. I could see that changing as existing programs grow and new ones are added. For instance, CBU's physician assistant program is very robust and likely to remain strong. Also, we're about to start a dental hygiene program, a four-year undergraduate program. We think that's going to be another popular program in the College of Health Science. We also expect upscaling in programs such as radiology and speech language pathology.

The social work program in the College of Behavioral and Social Science is going gangbusters. The Doctor of Social Work (DSW) program is one of the newest and larger doctoral programs at CBU. Along with the Master of Social Work, we think the DSW has a good run ahead. Additionally, we see continued strength in the 'pre-' programs, such as pre-law, pre-dent, pre-med, pre-vet, and more. Those are very robust. So are engineering, architecture, and aviation.

We are also looking at ways CBU can serve the region and help meet needs in underserved areas. One possibility involves healthcare, which is still a pressing need throughout the Inland Empire. Programs like those in the College of Health Science and College of Nursing position CBU as a potential provider of healthcare services that can be delivered in storefront settings or mobile clinics. In 2023, the College of Nursing launched CBU's first such mobile clinic to offer a range of services such as health screenings, immunizations, lab testing, diabetes care, and treatment for acute and chronic illnesses. An expanded version of this service would fit well with CBU's Great Commission focus. It would help meet the region's healthcare needs and could also serve as clinical training sites for students in health-related fields.

The decision we made years ago to add STEM programs to the academic mix at CBU was a game changer. Those programs fueled explosive enrollment growth and continue to attract students preparing to enter the labor force as well qualified graduates in the sciences, technology, engineering, and mathematics. The programs also contribute significantly to the institution's sustainability.

I think the enrollment mix at CBU is likely to change a little bit going forward, with graduate students increasing as a percentage of overall enrollment. I also see some shifting to higher margin graduate programs in health sciences, social work, and technical fields while maintaining steady traditional undergraduate numbers. To the outside person it probably would not look like much has changed, but internally the institution could be much stronger.

In my inaugural address nearly 30 years ago, I declared "We are ready" to meet the challenges facing a struggling Baptist college and I shared my vision to transform it into "a Great Commission University on the West Coast reaching out to the ends of the earth." The vision I laid out still applies; just replace 'college' with 'university' in the following excerpt:

> "During our tenure (I use the plural because the Presidency is a family endeavor, both immediate and College-wide), the College will be student centered. At the heart of all that the College attempts must be that which is best for the student. Cal Baptist will seek to produce graduates possessing an excellent academic preparation, a Biblically based morality and worldview, a passion for missions, a service mentality, and a strong work ethic.
>
> During our tenure, Cal Baptist will be in the arena contending. We will seek to attract trustees, friends,

> faculty, staff and students who believe passionately in the mission.
>
> We will seek those who can and will take California Baptist College to new heights, deeper strength, and broader service and influence. Removal of limitations, creative problem solving, energetic and enthusiastic pacing, and openness to new paradigms will be expected."

There is no crystal ball to divine what lies ahead for California Baptist University. Instead, there is a granite globe rotating atop a base inscribed with the text of the Great Commission. It's the Kugel in the breezeway of the Eugene and Billie Yeager Center. The Kugel symbolizes the theme that has permeated the culture and traditions of CBU since 1994. And it reminds us daily of the commitment at the heart of the CBU experience.

I believe California Baptist University will thrive long into the future if it will remain committed to its core values, if it will remain committed to serving people, and if it will be nimble, responsive to the market, and opportunistic. If it will do all that, the future is bright.

APPENDIX

Dr. Ronald L. Ellis | 30th Anniversary Timeline

1994

- On November 1, 1994, Dr. Ronald L. Ellis began serving as president at California Baptist College

1995

- Enrollment jumps from 808 in fall 1994 to 1,226 in fall 1995
- Evening School quadruples in size
- Master of Education added

1996

- Master of Business Administration added

1997

- International Service Projects launch with teams of students traveling to China, Ecuador and Russia

- Mission Hall and Lancer Fitness Complex constructed
- Baseball team wins Golden State Athletic Conference championship and makes appearance in the NAIA World Series

1998

- Lancer Aquatic Center completed
- California Baptist College becomes California Baptist University
- Men's cross country team wins Golden State Athletic Conference championship

1999

- Men's track (distance) team wins university's first national title at the NAIA Indoor Track & Field championship
- Men's volleyball inaugural team wins NAIA National Tournament championship
- Men's water polo play inaugural season

2000

- Men's cross country team wins Golden State Athletic Conference championship

2001

- Men's volleyball team wins NAIA championship

2002

- Shelby and Ferne Collinsworth School of Music founded

2003

- Eugene and Billie Yeager Center completed
- Dr. Bonnie G. Metcalf School of Education added

2004

- Ronald L. and Jane D. Ellis Great Commission Plaza constructed
- Master of Music added
- Women's tennis introduced
- Softball team makes first appearance in the NAIA World Series of Softball
- Men's volleyball team wins third NAIA national championship
- Women's volleyball team wins first NAIA national championship

2005

- The Cottages (on-campus housing) added
- JoAnn Hawkins Music Building opens
- School of Nursing established and received approval from the State of California Board of Registered Nursing
- Women's golf introduced
- Men's and women's volleyball teams win NAIA national championships
- Softball team wins NAIA Region II championship
- Women's swimming and diving teams capture NAIA national championship

2006

- Master of Public Administration added
- School of Nursing admits first students
- Men's golf and tennis teams added

- Men's volleyball team wins eighth NAIA national championship
- Men's and women's swimming and diving teams capture NAIA national championships

2007

- CBU-Rwanda Presidential Agreement established
- Lancer Outdoor Sports Complex completed
- School of Engineering opens
- Men's and women's swimming and diving teams win NAIA national championships
- Men's volleyball team wins NAIA championship
- Men's water polo team captures CWPA/NAIA national championship

2008

- Wrestling added to athletic teams
- Men's and women's swimming and diving teams capture NAIA national championships

2009

- United States Projects launch as extension to ISP
- Men's swimming and diving team captures NAIA national championship
- Softball team wins national championship

2010

- Division of Online and Professional Studies launched
- College of Allied Health opens
- Brisco's Cafe opens
- Summer of Service program begins

- CBU approved to join NCAA Division II, beginning three-year process
- CBU approved to join Pacific West Conference, with competition beginning 2011
- Men's volleyball team wins NAIA championship

2011

- CBU acquires Parkside Village apartments, renamed The Colony at CBU
- School of Engineering becomes College of Engineering
- CBU receives first ever 10-year accreditation from Western Association of Schools and Colleges
- Women's golf wins first NAIA national championship title
- Men's and women's soccer teams win National Christian College Athletic Association (NCCAA) championship
- Men's volleyball team wins NAIA national championship
- Women's volleyball team wins NCCAA championship
- Sports Spectrum names CBU the top Christian College athletics program

2012

- CBU claims PacWest Commissioner's Cup
- CBU wins NCCAA Presidential Award
- School of Business Building completed
- Recreation Center opens
- Women's soccer team wins PacWest and NCCAA championships; Men's team wins PacWest championship
- Men's cross country, baseball and softball teams win PacWest championships
- Women's swimming and diving team wins Scholar All-American Award
- Men's and women's track (distance) team members win NCCAA national championships

- Cheer team wins USA Collegiate Cheer championship
- International Service Projects celebrate 15th year

2013

- Tahquitz Pines gifted by Hobby Lobby
- Dr. Ellis selected as one of 25 most influential leaders in Riverside
- Aviation Science program introduced
- FedEx donates Boeing 727 to Aviation Science program
- Campus publications win first national awards
- Baseball team wins NCCAA World Series
- Wrestling team wins National Collegiate Wrestling Association championship
- Cheer team wins National Cheerleaders Association Cheer and Dance championship

2014

- Lancer Plaza North opens
- 400th team participates in the flagship International Service Projects, United States Projects and Summer of Service
- CBU claims PacWest Commissioner's Cup for second time in three years
- Dr. Ellis selected to serve on NCAA Division II President's Council
- CBU qualifies 12 teams for NCAA playoffs
- Chick-fil-A and Campus Xpress open
- CBU wins first NCAA Division II championship, places No. 26 nationally among D-II membership in Learfield Sports Directors' Cup final standings

2015

- College of Allied Health renamed College of Health Science
- College of Health Science dedicates new campus with more than 70,000 square feet under roof on more than 11 acres

2016

- School of Nursing becomes College of Nursing

2017

- 153,000-square-foot Events Center dedicated
- First doctoral degree granted
- The School of Behavioral Sciences officially transitions into College of Behavioral and Social Sciences
- CBU announces acceptance into Western Athletic Conference (WAC) and transition to NCAA Division I

2018

- 100,000-square-foot Dennis and Carol Troesh Engineering Building opens
- CBU Lancers begin competing in NCAA Division 1, Western Athletic Conference

2019

- Athletic Performance Center completed
- Five-story East Parking Structure opens
- New entrance to CBU opens at Adams Street and Lancer Lane
- International Service Projects celebrates 5,000 plus volunteers

2020

- CBU offers all online courses during spring semester in response to COVID-19
- Magnolia Crossing campus housing opens

2021

- CBU holds 12 in-person spring commencement ceremonies to honor 2021 and 2020 graduates
- Chronicle of Higher Education ranked CBU No. 7 among fastest-growing U.S. colleges (2009–2019)

2022

- NCAA board approves CBU's Division I membership status
- CBU combines the music and theatre programs in the Shelby and Ferne Collinsworth School of Performing Arts
- CBU Soccer Stadium completed
- Men's soccer wins its first WAC Championship and qualifies for the NCAA Division I tournament

2023

- CBU announces historic gift of $28.5 million and the naming of The Dale E. and Sarah Ann Fowler Events Center
- President Ronald L. Ellis, Ph.D. inducted into the Riverside Sport Hall of Fame
- Women's track members Greta Karinauskaite and Yasna Petrova compete in the National Championships and Greta brings home a silver medal in the 3,000 meter steeplechase
- Hae and Shina Park Building named — houses the Dr. Robert K. Jabs School of Business, Career Center and Innovators Auditorium

- CBU receives a $3 million grant from the U.S. Department of Education for a program aimed at improving higher education outcomes for Hispanic and low-income students
- Men's soccer becomes the WAC's first-ever back-to-back champions, advancing to the NCAA tournament and winning the first-round match against the University of San Diego
- Wall Street Journal ranks CBU No. 1 (tied) for best career preparation and No. 2 for best student experience in the country

2024

- Women's basketball earns a trip to the NCAA Tournament and March Madness
- STUNT wins its fourth-straight national championship and extends its winning streak to 80 straight wins since the program's inception
- Fall marks the start of 13 new program launches – two certificate programs, five undergraduate degrees, four master's degrees, and two doctoral programs
- CBU has nine doctoral programs and 600 doctoral students

Dr. Ronald L. Ellis Biography

Ronald L. Ellis, Ph.D. became the fifth president of California Baptist University on November 1, 1994. Since then, the institution has experienced sweeping changes in almost every facet of university life—from expanding academic programs to a successful athletics program.

Enrollment at CBU has grown by 1,377 percent during the Ellis presidency, from 808 in the fall of 1994 to 11,931 in the fall of 2024. During President Ellis' tenure, the university's operating budget has increased from $11.3 million to $397 million in FY25.

The NCAA Division I Board of Directors in 2022 granted CBU active status as a Division I institution, providing the Lancer athletics teams immediate eligibility for postseason play. Since then, CBU teams scored major accomplishments including: men's soccer became the first ever back-to-back Western Athletic Conference champions and competed in the NCAA Tournament; men's cross country was ranked fourth in the nation and both the men's and women's teams finished in the top 20 at the NCAA Division I championship; women's basketball won the WAC championship game and stamped their first-ever ticket to the March Madness tournament; swim and dive sent two athletes to the NCAA Championship; STUNT earned its fourth national championship; women's golf had a WAC

Tournament champion; and track and field brought home a silver medal at the National Championships.

Since the beginning of the four-year NCAA Division I transition, the Lancers have won 15 conference championships, logged 34 top-three conference finishes, and qualified 35 teams for postseason tournaments involving Division I programs. In 2020-21, women's basketball went undefeated during the regular season and the conference tournament. Other athletic accomplishments include winning the Pacific West Conference Commissioner's Cup six times and the NCAA Division II Learfield Directors Cup. President Ellis became the first leader of a PacWest member institution to serve on the NCAA Division II Presidents Council. His dedication to advancing sport at CBU earned him a special recognition in the Riverside Sport Hall of Fame Class of 2023.

New construction, renovation of existing facilities, and property acquisitions have dramatically transformed CBU's beautiful Southern California campus. The university has been the recipient of numerous beautification awards from the Keep Riverside Clean and Beautiful program. For the 19th consecutive year, U.S. News & World Report named CBU one of "America's Best Colleges" for 2025. CBU also was recognized by the Wall Street Journal as No. 1 in the country for career preparedness and No. 2 for best student experience.

Under the leadership of President Ellis, CBU has developed into a premier comprehensive Christian university, comprising 10 colleges and professional schools, offering more than 175 majors and minors as well as 41 graduate programs and nine doctoral programs.

President Ellis received a bachelor's degree from Houston Baptist University in 1977 and a master's degree in educational administration from Baylor University in 1981. In 1987, he completed a Ph.D. in higher education administration from Texas A&M University.

President Ellis and his wife, Jane Dowden Ellis, are active members of Magnolia Church in Riverside, where he has served as chair of the board of trustees. They have two sons and 14 grandchildren.

Dr. Mark A. Wyatt Biography

Dr. Mark A. Wyatt is vice president emeritus of California Baptist University. He served CBU as vice president for marketing and communication from 2002 until his retirement on January 31, 2020. Dr. Wyatt led the CBU professional staff responsible for branding, advertising, public relations, media relations, publications, and internet marketing activities. He also supervised the use of campus facilities by campus groups and external clients. Along with his administrative duties, Dr. Wyatt held the faculty rank of assistant professor of communication arts.

Prior to joining the CBU administration, Dr. Wyatt served more than 18 years as chief communications officer for California Southern Baptist Convention and editor of *The California Southern Baptist* newspaper. He has more than 50 years' experience in higher education administration, organizational communications, journalism, pastoral ministry and media including 14 years as a radio and television news reporter and anchor.

Dr. Wyatt was active in community affairs as an institutional representative for CBU on the International Relations Council for the City of Riverside and served as a director or member of two other non-profit organizations: The Riverside Arts Council; and the Greater Riverside Chambers of Commerce.

He is a 2004 graduate of the Riverside Chamber's acclaimed 'Leadership Riverside' program. He served as recording secretary for the Board of Directors of the International Association of Baptist Colleges and Universities and as national secretary of the Council for Christian Colleges and Universities' Commission for Public Relations Officers. He also was a member of the American Marketing Association–Inland Empire and is a lifetime member and former officer of the Baptist Communicators Association.

Dr. Wyatt earned a Doctor of Ministry in Executive Leadership from Golden Gate Baptist Theological Seminary in Mill Valley, California (now Gateway Seminary of the Southern Baptist Convention in Ontario, California); a Master of Divinity degree from The Southern Baptist Theological Seminary in Louisville, Kentucky; and a Bachelor of Fine Arts in Theatre Arts from Valdosta State University in Georgia.

Dr. Wyatt and his wife, Jean, have been married 53 years and reside in Riverside, California. They have three children and nine grandchildren.

Index

D

E

T

U

V

W

Y

Printed in the United States
by Baker & Taylor Publisher Services